D1627462

THE HONOURABLE
COMPANY OF
EDINBURGH GOLFERS
MUIRFIELD

Practice Ground

131ST OPEN CHAMPIONSHIP
Card of the Championship Course

Hole	Par	Yards	Hole	Par	Yards
1	4	448	10	4	475
2	4	351	11	4	389
3	4	378	12	4	381
4	3	213	13	3	191
5	5	560	14	4	448
6	4	468	15	4	415
7	3	185	16	3	186
8	4	443	17	5	546
9	5	508	18	4	449
Out	36	3,554	In	35	3,480
			Total	71	7,034

Hazleton Publishing Ltd
3 Richmond Hill, Richmond, Surrey TW10 6RE

Published 2002 by Hazleton Publishing Ltd
Copyright © 2002 The Championship Committee Merchandising Limited

Statistics of 131st Open Championship produced on a
Unisys Computer System

Assistance with records provided by Stewart McDougall and Salvatore Johnson.

Photographs on pages 9, 10, 12, 13 courtesy of Stephen Szurlej.
Photographs on pages 14, 17 courtesy of Fred Vuich.

A CIP catalogue record for this book is available
from the British Library

ISBN: 1-903135-18-4

Type and layout by Davis Design
Printed in Great Britain

The Open Championship 2002

WRITERS
Robert Sommers
Michael McDonnell
Marino Parascenzo
Andy Farrell
Ron Sirak
John Hopkins

PHOTOGRAPHERS
Michael Cohen
Phil Inglis

EDITOR
Bev Norwood

www.opengolf.com

Authorised by the Championship Committee of The Royal and Ancient Golf Club of St Andrews

The Championship Committee

CHAIRMAN

David Pepper

DEPUTY CHAIRMAN

Michael Grint

COMMITTEE

Michael Brown

John Roger Jones

Geoffrey Marks

Pat Montgomery

Richard Muckart

Dougal Rae

Colin Strachan

Peter Unsworth

Martin Yates

ADVISORY MEMBER

William Black

Council of National Golf Unions

SECRETARY

Peter Dawson

CHAMPIONSHIP SECRETARY

David Hill

RULES SECRETARY

David Rickman

Introduction

By David Pepper
Chairman of Championship Committee
The Royal and Ancient Golf Club of St Andrews

It would have been difficult to write a script for the final day's play of the 131st Open Championship which could have improved upon the drama which ensued and eventually resulted in Ernie Els being crowned a very worthy Champion Golfer for the year and winner of the Gold Medal.

After a very wet six weeks leading up to the Championship, Muirfield was greener and softer than it had been all year. Nevertheless, Colin Irvine and his staff provided us with a course in excellent condition which brought nothing but praise from the players and press alike for the way in which it had been set up.

Once more Muirfield provided a wonderful test of golf. Hardly changed since 1928, its subtle greens and comparatively wide fairways lined by thick rough took their toll and the wind and rain on Saturday did the rest.

The Championship Committee are most grateful to The Honourable Company of Edinburgh Golfers for the loan of their magnificent links course and their enthusiastic support for the Championship. Similarly we are indebted to the hundreds of volunteers who helped in so many ways to ensure the smooth running of all the qualifying rounds as well as making the Championship itself such a success.

Finally I would like to thank the journalists and photographers whose contributions in the following pages have helped to record what was indeed a memorable Open Championship.

David Pepper

Foreword

By Ernie Els

Ever since I have been playing this game, and that's been since I was eight years old, I have wanted to win the Open Championship. I have known the names of the champions, such as Gary Player here in 1959 and Jack Nicklaus in 1966, and I was here for the first time in 1992, playing four rounds as a 22-year-old. So I have had a dream of holding the claret jug for a long time.

As you might have known from my expression, it was an unbelievable experience. It was an unbelievable four days—plus five holes—really, and most of the time I played well. I was able to hang in there mentally and physically and just grind it out.

I didn't come to Muirfield with a lot of confidence, but I left as Open champion, and that was all that mattered. I had a lot of patience Saturday in the rain and windy conditions, and I carried that over to the final round. Then I went from almost a clear winner to almost a clear loser in the space of three or four holes, but I guess I had the staying power this time.

The last couple of years, I haven't been that good in playoffs, and on the 72nd hole I really wanted to birdie it. When I left that putt short and I signed my card, I was down in the dumps. I had some time to compose myself before the playoff, and I talked to my wife, Leizl, and Jos Vanstiphout, my sports psychologist. My attitude was that I had four holes to play, those were the most important holes of my career, and I was going to try 100 percent on each shot.

This was one of the hardest tournaments I have ever played, and it's the most rewarding. It is the greatest championship in the world, played in front of the greatest crowd in the world.

Ernie Els

No Tricks or Surprises Here

By Michael McDonnell

At the beginning of the last century, the eminent author and administrator John Low laid down a simple but profound definition of what he considered to be both the challenge and purpose of playing golf.

"Golf at its best," he decided, "should be a contest of risks. The heart of golf lies in propelling the ball from one situation to another. Each stretch of the journey should be hazardous; the links should be almost too difficult for the player."

As to the risk factor and its outcome, this venerable Scot could speak from painful experience, because in the semifinal of the 1897 Amateur Championship at Muirfield, his opponent, James Robb, was in danger of hitting out of bounds on three holes yet his golf ball remained in play each time and Low lost in extra holes.

Nonetheless, Low's philosophy was correct in that the element of risk lies central to every championship triumph. More than this, it is the ability to recognise the dangers, then summon the requisite courage and skill to overcome them, that elevates the champion from the rest, particularly on a links besieged by savage weather.

When Walter Hagen beheld the ferocity of the wind at Muirfield at the 1929 Open Championship, he knew there were tactical decisions to be made. In his autobiography he recalled "the blustering wind which swept across the links with challenging wildness" and temperatures so low that overcoats and gloves were required between shots and discarded only briefly at the green.

He chose what he called "the ground route" as the safest means round Muirfield, because a ball in the air had neither control nor distance, particularly when players were struggling to maintain a stance long enough to hit it. In the last two rounds he was paired with a very young Henry Cotton, who at that early stage of his career had no such tactical wisdom and was completely baffled by it all.

Yet Hagen was still prepared to take chances in an effort to break free from his rivals, and during both rounds on the final day ignored the designated right-

The third green is heavily protected to the front.

The fourth hole, lengthened by 33 yards, demands power as well as accuracy.

hand dogleg route of the eighth hole and simply took a direct shortcut into heather that yielded 3s both times yet could just as easily have found disaster. Even so, The Haig rode his good fortune to two rounds of 75 and earned his fourth Open title.

History suggests that in the 1972 championship Jack Nicklaus was not prepared to take such risks until it was too late. He had played with unusual caution by taking long irons from many tees for three rounds, as though fearful that the slightest diversion might cost him. Years later, Nicklaus revealed he also had suffered a stiff neck and could not swing freely until the last day.

He had already picked up the Masters and US Open earlier in the season, so the great achievement was tantalisingly close. But by the time he made his bid on the final day, others had occupied centre stage and Nicklaus finished one stroke behind Lee Trevino, the new champion.

To this day there is the nagging thought that more risk might have resulted in a different outcome. But then, such decisions and their consequences are always clearly identified at Muirfield because it is the most complete and honest examination of all the Open Championship courses. No tricks, hidden hazards, or surprises. As Nicklaus says, "What you see is what you get."

The course in fact forms two loops, with the front nine following a clockwise route outside the homeward loop, which more or less runs anticlockwise. This configuration means that a player must tackle the wind coming from all directions during the course of the round, and the stronger the gusts, the more inventive the stroke-making must become.

Moreover, it requires constant vigilance and focus until the very last putt is holed, because nothing can ever be taken for granted at Muirfield, particularly over the closing stretch. Henry Cotton was

Round Muirfield

No 1 448 Yards Par 4
A demanding start, especially into the prevailing wind, because the tee shot must be kept left to provide the best angle of attack along a fairway that sweeps gently to the right past bunkers short and right to the green.

No 2 351 Yards Par 4
The out of bounds stone wall flanking the left side and coming within 15 feet of the green dictates a more cautious strategy from the tee, and a long iron still leaves the undulating green within range of a gentle wedge shot. Big hitters can drive the green, but the risks are great.

No 3 378 Yards Par 4
The tee shot must find the correct position between two bunkered mounds which stand sentinel either side of the fairway. Best to be left to have a full view of the long green that rises towards the back and is heavily protected at the front.

No 4 213 Yards Par 3
This hole has been lengthened by 33 yards since the 1992 championship and demands power as well as accuracy from a raised tee to a plateau green that is guarded by bunkers at the front as well as grassy hollows on either side. It is essential to find the heart of the green because peripheral slopes carry the ball off the putting surface.

No 5 560 Yards Par 5
A crucial tee shot at a slight angle to the fairway over a string of five righthand bunkers. A more cautious shot to the left may still find trouble, and the entrance to this green, which is in range downwind for the stronger players, is narrowed by bunkers on either side.

No 6 468 Yards Par 4
Homework is required for the right line here from the tee, because the shot is played over the crest of the fairway and invariably in a crosswind, so past experience is essential. The fairway then sweeps down to the left and the hollow just short of the green makes the flag look closer than it really is.

No 7 185 Yards Par 3
An uphill tee shot into the prevailing wind with a steep slope and bunkers on the left to catch the stroke that is even fractionally tugged, and a solitary but seemingly magnetic bunker on the right for a pushed shot. The green slopes down from back to front and towards the left and is extremely exposed.

No 8 443 Yards Par 4
The tee shot is vital and, for all but the longest hitters, must be placed left of a cluster of bunkers which guard this righthand dogleg, leaving a relatively simple shot over more bunkers short of the green which slopes away to the rear.

No 9 508 Yards Par 5
The landing area for the tee shot, invariably played into the prevailing wind, is placed narrowly between a deep lefthand bunker and heavy rough to the right. Most players avoid the risk and take three shots to reach the green that is close to the out of bounds on its left.

No 10 475 Yards Par 4
Righthand bunkers catch the tee shot that drifts on the wind at a particularly narrow part of this fairway. A ridge with two bunkers runs across the fairway 100 yards from the green and slightly obstructs a proper view of the shot required between two bunkers to reach the green.

No 11 389 Yards Par 4
More homework is needed for the line of the tee shot over the crest of this hill to a fairly generous fairway on the other side with a bunker on the right side and another strategically placed on the left. The green is small and heavily protected on all sides by deep bunkers.

No 12 381 Yards Par 4
Proper positioning from the tee is essential and more important than distance, because the second shot has to be played to a long, narrow green that is heavily bunkered on both sides and slopes towards the rear.

No 13 191 Yards Par 3
An extra 32 yards have been added since the 1992 championship and increased the difficult of this uphill hole. The green is long but extremely narrow and slopes off towards the left. It is heavily bunkered and also falls from the back towards the front.

No 14 448 Yards Par 4
An elevated tee invariably into the prevailing wind makes placement crucial between or beyond bunkers on either side of the fairway, and the approach, sometimes with a long iron, has to find a plateau green that slopes away on all sides and has a front edge bunker.

No 15 415 Yards Par 4
A tee shot—preferably with a long iron to take the bunkers on either side of the fairway out of play—sets up the safe approach on the righthand dogleg to a large, undulating green which, because of its expanse, can present putting problems.

No 16 186 Yards Par 3
Absolute precision is needed on the tee shot, because a ball hitting the left side of the green is likely to slide off into bunkers or the rough. Not a good plan to attack the flag position, but wiser to play for the centre of the green and trust the putter.

No 17 546 Yards Par 5
A cluster of bunkers on the left of this lefthand dogleg dictate that the tee shot must be directed to the right, and the green is tucked protectively behind gentle sand hills and can only be reached via a narrow entrance.

No 18 449 Yards Par 4
Bunkers on the left menace the tee shot, but the righthand bunker threatens the safety shot, and bunkers short of the green foil the fainthearted approach to this sharply rising, sloping green that is heavily trapped on either side.

A ridge runs across the 10th fairway 100 yards from the green.

bunkered at the last hole and failed to get out at his first attempt, but coolly averted the prospect of a deepening crisis to win the 1948 title. Gary Player spent an agonising vigil waiting for others to overtake him after he took 6 on the same hole in 1959, but then discovered that he was beyond everybody's reach.

In 1966 David Thomas, who twice finished runnerup in the Open, confessed that his mind strayed to "the Aston Martin" and other rewards that victory would bring, until he too succumbed over the closing stretch as Nicklaus became champion. Perhaps there was little doubt in Tony Jacklin's mind that he would become the new champion in 1972 when his closest rival, Lee Trevino, found trouble on the 71st hole and was through the back of the green in 4, while Jacklin was on the green in 3. But a spectacular chip-in by the American completely devastated Jacklin, who crumbled and, by his own admission, was never the same competitor again.

For many years a newspaper cartoon hung in the entrance hall of The Honourable Company of Edinburgh Golfers clubhouse with the message "Muirfield welcomes careful drivers." It was a memento of

The 11th green is small and heavily protected by deep bunkers.

Reachable by a narrow entrance, the 17th green is tucked protectively behind gentle sand hills.

the 1966 championship, when the rough was so high the fairways looked like corridors cut through it, and the joke may have obscured the underlying message that shotmaking and not brute force decides a championship over this particular test.

More to the point, links golf has always been a personal battle with the elements and not simply a test of comparative skills. When Tom Watson won in 1980, the first round was beset by wind and a continuous downpour. In 1987 the winds gusted to 40 miles an hour, and Jack Nicklaus, Tom Kite, Scott Simpson, and Mark O'Meara all scored in the 80s. That said, it is an undeniable fact of championship golf that no matter how bad the conditions may become, somebody always "finds a way."

Thus it is totally fitting that one of the great players renowned for his judicious approach to the game should have prevailed at Muirfield in that championship and also in the one that followed in 1992.

Nick Faldo exerted an iron self-control that extended not only to his play but also to his emotions in the heat of battle. In the final round of the 1987 event, he put together 18 pars, not all of them textbook, to win the title. In 1992 his chance seemed to be slipping away through a series of errors when he suddenly snapped out of his decline with what he later described as "the best four holes of my life" that included two birdies and steered him to the title.

The measure of a course must be gauged by the calibre of its champions, and a roll of honour that includes Harry Vardon, James Braid, Ted Ray, Walter Hagen, Alf Perry, Henry Cotton, Gary Player, Jack Nicklaus, Lee Trevino, Tom Watson, Nick Faldo—and now Ernie Els—suggests that The Honourable Company of Edinburgh Golfers has played an integral part in golf's evolving history ever since its rules of the game were devised in 1744.

Exempt Competitors

Name, Country	Category
Robert Allenby, Australia	4, 14
Stephen Ames, Trinidad & Tobago	16
Billy Andrade, USA	1, 4
Stuart Appleby, Australia	17
Warren Bennett, England	9
John Bickerton, England	9
Thomas Bjorn, Denmark	4, 5, 18
Angel Cabrera, Argentina	4, 5
Mark Calcavecchia, USA	3, 4, 14, 18
Michael Campbell, New Zealand	4, 5
Jim Carter, USA	16
Paul Casey, England	9
Alex Cejka, Germany	1
Roger Chapman, England	8
K.J. Choi, South Korea	15
Stewart Cink, USA	4, 18
Tim Clark, South Africa	24
Darren Clarke, N. Ireland	1, 4, 5, 18
Jose Coceres, Argentina	4
John Cook, USA	4
John Daly, USA	2, 4
Chris DiMarco, USA	4, 14
Bradley Dredge, Wales	8
Joe Durant, USA	14
David Duval, USA	1, 2, 4, 13, 14, 18
Ernie Els, South Africa	1, 4, 5, 10, 14
Bob Estes, USA	4, 14
Gary Evans, England	8
Nick Faldo, England	2
Marc Farry, France	9
Niclas Fasth, Sweden	1, 4, 5, 18
Brad Faxon, USA	4, 14
Darren Fichardt, South Africa	8
Pierre Fulke, Sweden	18
Jim Furyk, USA	4, 14, 18
Sergio Garcia, Spain	1, 4, 14, 18
Ricardo Gonzalez, Argentina	9
Retief Goosen, South Africa	1, 4, 5, 10
Mathias Gronberg, Sweden	5
Anders Hansen, Denmark	6
Soren Hansen, Denmark	8
Padraig Harrington, Ireland	4, 5, 18
Dudley Hart, USA	4
Scott Hoch, USA	4, 14, 18
David Howell, England	5

Name, Country	Category
Mikko Ilonen, Finland	1
Toshimitsu Izawa, Japan	4, 23
Fredrik Jacobson, Sweden	8
Raphael Jacquelin, France	1
Thongchai Jaidee, Thailand	21
Lee Janzen, USA	10
Miguel Angel Jimenez, Spain	1, 5
Steve Jones, USA	10
Robert Karlsson, Sweden	5
Shingo Katayama, Japan	4, 23
Jonathan Kaye, USA	16
Jerry Kelly, USA	4
Kenichi Kuboya, Japan	26
Matt Kuchar, USA	4
Neal Lancaster, USA	17
Barry Lane, England	7
Bernhard Langer, Germany	1, 4, 5, 18
*Alejandro Larrazabal, Spain	28
Paul Lawrie, Scotland	2, 5
Scott Laycock, Australia	22
Stephen Leaney, Australia	9
Tom Lehman, USA	2, 4, 14
Justin Leonard, USA	2, 4
Thomas Levet, France	5
Frank Lickliter II, USA	14
Peter Lonard, Australia	16
Davis Love III, USA	4, 12, 14, 18
Sandy Lyle, Scotland	3
Malcolm Mackenzie, England	7
Jeff Maggert, USA	16
Shigeki Maruyama, Japan	4

It's a Fact

Thirty-seven citizens of the United Kingdom have won the Open Championship, more than any other nationality. There have been 24 champions from the United States, four from Australia, three from South Africa (including 2002), and one each from Argentina, France, New Zealand, Spain, and Zimbabwe.

Name, Country	Category	Name, Country	Category
Len Mattiace, USA	4	Chris Riley, USA	17
Billy Mayfair, USA	1	Loren Roberts, USA	1
Scott McCarron, USA	4	Eduardo Romero, Argentina	7
Paul McGinley, Ireland	4, 5, 18	Justin Rose, England	24
Rocco Mediate, USA	4	Adam Scott, Australia	4, 5
Phil Mickelson, USA	4, 14, 18	Vijay Singh, Fiji	1, 4, 11, 12, 14
Kiyoshi Miyazato, Japan	23	Chris Smith, USA	16
Colin Montgomerie, Scotland	1, 4, 5, 6, 18	Des Smyth, Ireland	1
Tsuneyuki Nakajima, Japan	26	Jamie Spence, England	9
Greg Norman, Australia	2	Ian Stanley, Australia	27
Peter O'Malley, Australia	5, 22	Steve Stricker, USA	17
Mark O'Meara, USA	2, 11	Kevin Sutherland, USA	1, 4
Jose Maria Olazabal, Spain	4, 11	Hal Sutton, USA	13, 18
Andrew Oldcorn, Scotland	6	Toru Suzuki, Japan	26
Greg Owen, England	7	Toru Taniguchi, Japan	26
Jesper Parnevik, Sweden	1, 4, 18	Taichi Teshima, Japan	20
Craig Parry, Australia	22	David Toms, USA	4, 12, 14, 18
Corey Pavin, USA	10	Bob Tway, USA	17
Craig Perks, New Zealand	13	Scott Verplank, USA	4, 14, 18, 19
(WD)Kenny Perry, USA	4	Duffy Waldorf, USA	17
Tim Petrovic, USA	16	Tom Watson, USA	3
Carl Pettersson, Sweden	7	Mike Weir, Canada	4, 14
Ian Poulter, England	8	Lee Westwood, England	18
Nick Price, Zimbabwe	2, 4	Dean Wilson, USA	23
Phil Price, Wales	18	Tiger Woods, USA	2, 4, 10, 11, 12, 13, 14, 18
Jean-Francois Remesy, France	9	Ian Woosnam, Wales	1, 5
John Riegger, USA	17	* Denotes amateurs (WD) Withdrew	

Final Qualifiers

Dunbar
*Simon Young, England, 66-68–134
Patrik Sjoland, Sweden, 65-69–134
Luke Donald, England, 67-69–136
Esteban Toledo, Mexico, 67-69–136
Steve Elkington, Australia, 67-70–137
Mattias Eliasson, Sweden, 66-71–137
Ian Garbutt, England, 67-70–137

Gullane No. 1
James Kingston, South Africa, 64-67–131
Fredrik Andersson, Sweden, 62-69–131
Adam Mednick, Sweden, 64-69–133
John Senden, Australia, 66-67–133
Raymond Russell, Scotland, 65-68–133
(P)Richard Green, Australia, 64-70–134
(P)Gary Emerson, England, 66-68–134

Luffness New
Benn Barham, England, 65-68–133
Andrew Coltart, Scotland, 61-72–133
*John Kemp, England, 65-68–133
Peter Baker, England, 65-68–133
Paul Eales, England, 65-69–134
Magnus Persson, Sweden, 66-68–134
Jarrod Moseley, Australia, 68-66–134

North Berwick
Scott Henderson, Scotland, 65-68–133
Paul Mayoh, England, 69-66–135
Trevor Immelman, South Africa, 63-72–135
Matthew Cort, England, 66-69–135
(P)David Park, Wales, 66-70–136
(P)Roger Wessels, South Africa, 67-69–136
(W)Tom Whitehouse, England, 68-68–136

* Denotes amateurs   (P) Qualified after playoff
(W) Qualified when Kenny Perry withdrew

The Honourable Company of Edinburgh Golfers were host to their 15th Open Championship.

Key to Exemptions from Regional and Final Qualifying

Exemptions for 2002 were granted to the following:

(1) First 15 and anyone tying for 15th place in the 2001 Open Championship.

(2) The Open Champions 1992-2001.

(3) Past Open Champions aged 65 or under on 21 July 2002.

(4) The first 50 players on the Official World Golf Ranking as at 30 May 2002.

(5) First 20 in the Official Money List of the PGA European Tour for 2001.

(6) The Volvo PGA Champions for 1999-2002.

(7) First 5 and anyone tying for 5th place, who are not otherwise exempt, in the top 20 of the Official Money List of the PGA European Tour for 2002 at 30 May.

(8) First 7 and anyone tying for 7th place, who are not otherwise exempt, in the top 25 of a cumulative money list taken from all official PGA European Tour events from the Volvo PGA Championship up to and including The Scottish Open at Loch Lomond.

(9) The leading 8 players not otherwise exempt having applied (8) above, in The 2002 Scottish Open at Loch Lomond. Ties for last place or places will be decided by the better final round score and, if still tied, by the better third round score and then by the better second round score. If still tied, all players thus still tying will be deemed exempt under this category.

Note: Those players who appeared in the draw for Rounds 3 & 4 of The Scottish Open at Loch Lomond were ineligible to compete in the Final Qualifying Competition.

(10) The US Open Champions for 1993-2002.

(11) The US Masters Champions for 1998-2002.

(12) The USPGA Champions for 1997-2001.

(13) The USPGA Tour Players Champions for 1999-2002.

(14) First 20 on the Official Money List of the USPGA Tour for 2001.

(15) First 5 and anyone tying for 5th place, not otherwise exempt, in the top 20 of the Official Points Standing of the USPGA Tour for 2002 at 30 May.

(16) First 7 and anyone tying for 7th place, not otherwise exempt, in the top 25 of a cumulative money list taken from the USPGA Tour Players Championship and the 5 USPGA Tour events leading up to and including the Advil Western Open.

(17) The leading 8 players not otherwise exempt having applied (16) above, in the 2002 Advil Western Open. Ties for last place or places will be decided by the better total round score and, if still tied, by the better third round score and then by the better second round score. If still tied, all players thus still tying will be deemed exempt under this category.

(18) Selected members of the 2001 Ryder Cup teams.

(19) The Canadian Open Champion for 2001.

(20) The Japan Open Champion for 2001.

(21) First place on the Asian PGA Davidoff Tour for 2001.

(22) First 3 and anyone tying for 3rd place on the Tour of Australasia for 2001/2002.

(23) First 3 and anyone tying for 3rd place on the Japan Golf Tour for 2001.

(24) First 2 and anyone tying for 2nd place on the Southern Africa PGA Sunshine Tour for 2001/2002.

(25) The leading player, not otherwise exempt, in the 2002 Mizuno Open.

(26) First 4 and anyone tying for 4th place, who are not otherwise exempt having applied (25) above, in the top 20 of a cumulative money list taken from all official Japan Golf Tour events from the Japan PGA Championship up to and including the Mizuno Open.

(27) The Senior British Open Champion for 2001.

(28) The Amateur Champion for 2002.

(29) The USA Amateur Champion for 2001.

(30) The European Individual Amateur Champion for 2001.

Note: Exemption for performance as an Amateur under (28) to (30) inclusive would only be granted if the Competitor concerned was still an Amateur on 18 July 2002.

Woods Begins His Quest

By Robert Sommers

Forty-nine years before the world's best golfers assembled at Muirfield, about 20 miles east of Edinburgh, the Open Championship took on even further significance.

As the oldest of all the golf championships, it had always drawn the game's select players, except for the grim depression years of the 1930s and the lingering austerity period following the Second World War. Then in 1953 Ben Hogan won both the Masters Tournament and the US Open and announced he would enter the Open Championship for the first time, because, he was told, his record would not be complete unless at least once he held the game's oldest trophy.

By then the Masters had climbed past the North and South and the Western Opens, which had been more significant before the war. With golf rejuvenated and the skilful promotional drive of the Augusta National Golf Club at work, the Masters joined the game's elite competitions, even though it allowed only a limited field generously laced with champions of the past.

Tiger Woods was trying to make history.

Hogan won the 1953 Open at Carnoustie, of course, and set a standard no one had matched. Since then, no one has won those three events in the same year.

In 1960 Arnold Palmer set a goal of winning not only those three, but the USPGA Championship as well, but Kel Nagle defeated him by a stroke at St Andrews, ending his dream. It had been Palmer's vision that those four tournaments should comprise a Grand Slam, the professional equivalent of the achievement of Bob Jones in 1930, when Jones won the Open and Amateur championships of Britain and the United States.

Jack Nicklaus was the second, after Palmer, to arrive at the Open with the thought of capturing all four in one year. When Nicklaus came to Muirfield in 1972 after winning both the Masters and US Open, he failed as well, beaten by Lee Trevino, again by one stroke.

Now, in 2002, Tiger Woods would give it a try. Like Palmer and Nicklaus before him, he came to the Open after having won both the Masters and US Opens in grand style, and also like Palmer and Nicklaus, he was without question the best player of the time.

Woods began his quest for the 2002 Open at 9.01 Thursday morning, grouped with Justin Rose, the 21-year-old South African-born Englishman, and the ir-

Excerpts from the
Press

"Tiger Woods was dressed like a curate eager to impress his bishop on a church outing. He had a white roll-neck shirt to provide a clerical collar, a black sleeveless sweater and dark grey trousers cut in the full, aldermanic style. Not that there was much priestly about his demeanour on the first tee after a cameraman clicked at the wrong time."

—David Davies, *The Guardian*

"If Woods wins by a stroke or two, muscling that 60-degree wedge onto the first fairway from that knee-high rough may be remembered as the most important shot he hit all week."

—Dave Anderson,
The New York Times

"Where Woods is young, sleek and sophisticated, Duffy Waldorf is middle-aged, well-built and clad in loud clothing."

—Mike Aitken, *The Scotsman*

"Sandy Lyle and Des Smyth may be in the autumn of their careers but there was a spring in their step when they walked off Muirfield yesterday."

—Neil McLeman, *Daily Record*

"With so much so-called smart money resting on their shoulders, it's a minor wonder that Padraig Harrington and Sergio Garcia could even haul themselves around the links."

—John Greechan, *Daily Mail*

Peter Baker (top) was first off, followed by Des Smyth (bottom left), and Sandy Lyle was in the second group.

Deadly serious while he plays, Shigeki Maruyama is otherwise known for his cheerful disposition.

repressible Japanese golfer Shigeki Maruyama. Woods was, of course, expected to give both his companions a lesson in course management, but in one of the game's rarer twists, Woods finished with the highest score of his grouping. He shot 70 while both Rose and Maruyama, along with 10 others, shot 68s, just one stroke off the 18-hole lead.

David Toms, the 2001 USPGA champion, shot 67 and shared first place with another American, Duffy Waldorf, and Carl Pettersson, a burly Swede who lives in the United States and commutes to PGA European Tour events.

Muirfield played about as easy as it could. The weather had been fair Monday, with clear skies and warm temperatures, but clouds had moved in Tuesday and carried over to Wednesday, bringing with them occasional rain, which softened the greens somewhat and lowered temperatures.

Thursday began warmer, and by mid-day the clouds had drifted off, the temperature climbed to 17°C, and the scores dropped. At the end of the day, 37 men had broken Muirfield's par of 71, and 22 of them had shot in the 60s.

Among those a stroke off the lead, Des Smyth was closing in on his 50th birthday, and 44-year-old Sandy Lyle, the 1985 Open champion, had suddenly found his game after years of struggle.

Phil Mickelson was among them as well, and so were 45-year-old Nick Price, eighth in the US Open, Soren Hansen, another Swede who would be in it to the end, Thomas Bjorn, who had tied for second at St Andrews in 2000 yet missed the cut the following year, and Steve Jones, the 1996 US Open champion, who would have joined the leaders had he not missed a putt from five feet on the home hole.

After shooting 69, Padraig Harrington remarked,

Thomas Bjorn was one off the lead despite this errant tee shot at the ninth.

David Duval wasn't sharp in his defence.

"There's not a hole out there you couldn't birdie if you were playing well. The toughest job is selecting the club for the tee shot."

Perhaps, but strange things happened nonetheless.

Hacking his way through Muirfield's legendary rough, Bjorn reeled off 3s on 10 holes, three of them on the first three, yet beat par by only three strokes. His first two birdies rated as remarkable. From the left rough on the first he pitched out to 20 feet and holed for a birdie, from the right rough on the second he pitched to 40 feet and holed another. His loose driving cost him on the sixth, though. In deep grass,

THURSDAY WEATHER
Temperature: low 10°C, high 17°C.
Light easterly to southerly breeze.

Robert Allenby (far right) leads amateur Alejandro Larrazabal and Jerry Kelly up the 13th fairway.

he couldn't reach the green and bogeyed.

Still, he did better than David Duval, the defender, and Shingo Katayama, who were with him. Both shot 72. Duval played every bit as well as Bjorn, yet had none of Bjorn's luck. Aside from seldom holing a putt, his pitch to save par on the 186-yard 16th hit the flagstick and caromed yards away. Instead of the 3 that seemed likely, Duval bogeyed. He'd had a similar incident early in the year, when an approach shot at Bay Hill, in Florida, deflected off the flagstick into a pond.

Putting for a birdie on one side of the 10th, Nick Faldo gave his ball too much punch, rolled it completely across the green, off the other side, and almost into a bunker. His next shot was a chip. He bogeyed and shot 73.

Then there was Thomas Levet on the ninth. He ripped a drive into the right rough, hacked his ball across the fairway into the left rough, spent several minutes find-

Anyone seen Jesper Parnevik?

Chopping hay off the 18th fairway, Jean-Francois Remesy (above) bogeyed to shoot 68, the same score as Len Mattiace (right).

ing it, walked forward to check the lay of the land for his third shot, then couldn't find his ball once again. After a frantic search, he found it before his allotted five minutes had run out, pitched out, chipped onto the green, and one-putted to save his par 5.

While all this was going on, most of the gallery's interest centred around Woods. He was indeed sailing into largely uncharted waters, and his day didn't begin too well. Setting himself to play his opening tee shot, Woods heard the click of a camera shutter. Stepping away, he said something to the photographer, then pushed his iron into the right rough.

Setting himself once again for a difficult recovery from deep grass, Woods heard the camera click once more and stepped away again. That was enough. Officials escorted the photographer off the grounds and temporarily stripped him of his credentials. It turned out that he had been hired by a magazine, and had worked at golf tournaments previously, but was so nervous at being at his first Open, he was clicking his camera accidentally.

That settled, Woods pulled out his 60-degree wedge, took a mighty whack as if scything hay, and somehow chopped the ball to the fairway. He claimed later he had hoped for no worse than a 5, but he pitched to six feet and saved a par 4.

Speaking of that remarkable recovery, Woods claimed later, "I don't

For Woods, An Opportunity Slips Away

Sometimes the grandest of dreams are shaken rudely awake by the most minute of moments. Such was the case for Tiger Woods, who backed off his first tee shot when disturbed by a photographer and then proceeded to launch a wayward two iron that nearly found the tented village to the right of the first fairway.

That Woods recovered from the thigh-high rough to save par and then displayed superb ball-striking throughout the day on his way to 70, one under par and three strokes off the lead, was impressive indeed. Certainly, Woods was well-positioned after one round in his quest to become the only man besides Ben Hogan to follow up victories in the Masters and the US Open with a triumph in the Open Championship.

"You can only shoot yourself out of the tournament the first day, and I certainly didn't do that," Woods said. "I got myself where I needed to be."

Still, the day was filled with ominous omens indicating his bid to sweep the four major professional championships in the same calendar year would encounter formidable obstacles. As well as Woods struck the ball—he hit 11 of 14 fairways and of the four greens he missed, two were on the fringe—he also used the putter 34 times (once from the fringe),

and the number of times his ball flirted with the hole, only to saunter past, hinted at frustration to come.

"I had six or seven lip-outs for birdie today," Woods said. "If those go in, it would have been a pretty good round." And if there was a day when he needed them to go in, it was on this windless day when the sun reflected off the glass-smooth Firth of Forth. This was a day to take the score low at Muirfield, and there was a distinct feeling in the still air that Woods had let an opportunity slip away.

"It was frustrating in the sense that I was hitting beautiful putts and they were lipping out," Woods said. "When you have good speed on the high side they generally go in. Today they were lipping out on the high side with good pace."

The first round appeared to be a feeling out process for Woods. It was as if he were testing his game plan on the venerable old links, seeing what modifications he needed to make. Using the driver only three times, Woods manoeuvred his way round Muirfield with the deft touch of a surgeon.

Both of his birdies on the first nine were of the two-putt variety on the par-5 fifth and ninth holes. He made bogeys on the sixth, when he missed a four-foot par putt after a 20-foot birdie try, and on No 10 when he drove into the right rough. He followed that bogey with a birdie on the next hole and then made pars on the final seven holes.

"If you shoot four solid rounds under par, more likely you're going to have a chance to win the tournament," Woods said. However, that more was not made of his round in perfect scoring conditions might have been the most ominous foreshadowing of all.

—Ron Sirak

know how I did that. I didn't think I could get to the fairway. I hit it as hard as I could. I could have hit it a foot or so or it could have gone as far as it went. It came out great."

From there on, even though Woods played his shots, he agonised through a frustrating day. The putts that had usually fallen for him either grazed the holes or stopped inches short. He birdied the fifth and ninth, two par 5s, and the 11th, a par 4, and dropped strokes on the sixth, a tough par 4 where he three-putted from 20 feet, and the 10th, where once again he drove into deep rough.

As usual, his ball-striking could hardly have been better. He missed only three fairways, and while statisticians claim he missed four greens, his approach to the 15th ran only a few inches onto the back collar.

At 70, Woods lay only three strokes behind the leaders, and with three rounds to play, no one ahead of him began counting their winnings. Strange things could happen, of course, but while Toms, the current USPGA champion, could become a serious threat, Waldorf and Pettersson didn't appear to have the background.

Actually, someone had written early in the week that Duffy Waldorf would not win the Open. But as Waldorf

First Round Leaders

HOLE	1	2	3	4	5	6	7	8	9	10	11	12	13	14	15	16	17	18	TOTAL
PAR	4	4	4	3	5	4	3	4	5	4	4	4	3	4	4	3	5	4	TOTAL
Duffy Waldorf	4	4	4	3	5	4	3	4	(4)	4	4	(3)	3	(3)	4	3	5	(3)	67
David Toms	4	4	(3)	(2)	5	4	3	4	5	4	4	(3)	(2)	[5]	4	3	(4)	4	67
Carl Pettersson	4	4	(3)	3	(2)	4	3	4	(4)	4	(3)	4	3	[5]	(3)	3	(4)	[5]	67
Des Smyth	[5]	4	4	3	(4)	(3)	3	4	5	4	(3)	4	3	4	4	3	(4)	4	68
Sandy Lyle	4	(3)	(3)	[4]	5	4	[4]	4	5	4	(3)	4	[4]	4	4	(2)	(4)	(3)	68
Shigeki Maruyama	4	(3)	4	3	(4)	4	3	(3)	(4)	4	4	4	3	[5]	4	3	5	4	68
Justin Rose	4	(3)	(3)	3	5	4	3	4	(3)	[5]	4	4	3	4	4	3	5	4	68
Thomas Djorn	(3)	(3)	(3)	3	5	[5]	3	(3)	5	(3)	[5]	(3)	3	4	4	3	[6]	4	68
Jean-Francois Remesy	[5]	(3)	4	(2)	5	[5]	3	4	(4)	4	4	(3)	(2)	[5]	(3)	3	(4)	[5]	68
Steve Jones	4	4	4	[4]	(4)	4	3	4	(4)	4	4	4	3	4	(3)	3	(3)	[5]	68
Len Mattiace	(3)	4	4	3	5	[5]	3	4	(4)	(3)	4	4	3	[5]	(3)	3	(4)	4	68
Nick Price	4	(3)	4	3	[6]	[5]	3	(3)	5	4	(3)	(3)	3	4	4	3	(4)	4	68
Phil Mickelson	4	4	[5]	3	5	4	(2)	4	5	4	4	4	(2)	4	4	3	(4)	(3)	68
Stephen Ames	[5]	(3)	[5]	3	5	4	3	[5]	(4)	4	(3)	4	(2)	[5]	4	(2)	(4)	(3)	68
Soren Hansen	4	(3)	4	[4]	(4)	4	3	4	(4)	4	4	4	(2)	4	4	3	(4)	[5]	68

From left, Stephen Ames and Soren Hansen were on 68 with 1994 champion Nick Price (bottom right).

Few could help but notice as Duffy Waldorf, sharing the lead with 67, cut a path through Muirfield.

pointed out Thursday, "He didn't say, he may not lead the Open." True enough, but then Duffy's record didn't strike fear into anyone's heart. A husky Californian a month away from his 40th birthday, he had won only four tournaments over a career dating back to 1987.

Unaffected, Waldorf takes a philosophical approach—he does own a degree in psychology from the University of California at Los Angeles. "About 12 years ago I realised that playing bad golf didn't make you a bad person. It's important to find that out," he said.

Driving mainly with irons and striking the ball not well but straight, Waldorf ran off eight consecutive pars before scoring his first birdie, holing from five feet on the ninth. Out in 35, one under par, he came back in 32 with five 3s on the home nine. He birdied the downhill 12th with a pitch to five feet. Tearing a seven-iron shot from the rough to

Low Scores	
Low First Nine	
Shigeki Maruyama	32
Justin Rose	32
Low Second Nine	
Mark O'Meara	31
Stephen Ames	31
Low Round	
Duffy Waldorf	67
David Toms	67
Carl Pettersson	67

Duffy Makes a
Colourful Splash

By Marino Parascenzo

"I don't want this to sound nasty," said a golf writer in the crowd, "but earlier this week somebody from the British press said Duffy Waldorf will not win a British Open at Muirfield ..."

A huge smile cut across Waldorf's beefy face, as though some graffiti artist had attacked his portrait. "He may be right," Waldorf conceded. "He didn't say that he may not lead at the Open."

In a world of smooth, tailored and solemn golfers, this was Duffy Waldorf, a jolly American with a round face and a quick and easy smile, noted for his good taste in wine, bad taste in clothes.

He has about 2,000 bottles in his cellar, many French and Californian wines, although his focus recently has been on Italian reds and Australian whites. Then there's his wardrobe. Golf shirts and caps, unmatched and maybe unmatchable. He makes Jesper Parnevik look like Saville Row. He appears to get dressed in the dark.

Waldorf was clad this Thursday in a shirt of white things swirling against a blue background—"Looks like Hawaiian flowers to me," he offered—and a blue cap with what looked like white streaks.

He was in the coveted interview seat in the press tent. He was jovial and comfortable. He was the early leader in the first round with a no-bogey, four-under-par 67. He would be tied later in the day, but for now, the stage was all his, and he loved it.

The soft insult? Someone thought he couldn't win the Open? So what else is new? Waldorf, at the age of 39, had long since rid himself of any delusions about his abilities. Back in his college days, he thought he was pretty hot stuff. Then he discovered the "real world" professors like to talk about. It hurt.

"When you get out on the pro tour, you find the conditions are a lot more difficult and the players are a lot better," Waldorf said. "It took me awhile to get used to that and to really raise my game." That is what he did in the first round of the Open. He patiently made his way to eight consecutive pars starting out.

Muirfield, with its mean rough and tight doglegs, dictated some odd club combinations, and Waldorf used one of the more interesting combinations on the par-5 ninth. He took a three iron off the tee, then a three wood to the green. It just missed. No matter. He chipped to five feet and sank the birdie putt.

He got three more birdies on the second nine. At the 12th hole, he hit a three iron and sand wedge combination, and holed a five-foot putt. At the 14th, it was another three iron off the tee and a magnificent seven iron out of the rough to one foot. At the 18th, he hit a two iron off the tee and a five iron to 18 feet, and dropped the putt for the 67, his best score ever in his five Opens.

In his four previous Opens, Waldorf had finished tied for 25th in 1992 at Muirfield, tied for 39th in 1993 at Sandwich, then after a long lapse, tied for 43rd in 1999 at Carnoustie, and tied for 54th last year at Royal Lytham & St Annes. Things suddenly looked encouraging, but Waldorf, with four victories in his 16 years on the PGA Tour, wasn't about to get excited over his 67.

"I was happy with my play, but I really didn't feel I was hitting it that solidly. But I was hitting it straight," Waldorf said. "I played fairly conservatively. I hit a lot of irons off the tee, and most of my irons were starting in the middle of the green. If you had seen me play bunkers a couple of days ago, you would aim for the middle of the greens, too."

No matter the golf, though, Waldorf spends more time explaining his wardrobe and his laid-back approach to life and golf. "If I had to rate my career according to how many wins I have and how I do in tournaments, I probably would be a pretty unhappy guy," he said. "But I don't look at it that way."

Having made his peace with the reality that he's not Jack Nicklaus, Arnold Palmer, nor Tiger Woods, he settled for being the best Duffy Waldorf can be. "You have to be able to separate things and evaluate your game in a safe place, and not have it affect your life," he said.

Waldorf took to wearing Hawaiian-style shirts, and caps that often bear no resemblance to the shirts. Someone reminded him of the shirt and cap he was wearing.

"This is one of the few days," Waldorf said, almost embarrassed by his accidental near-triumph, "where they get together."

One that slipped away in a round of 67 was this birdie try on the 16th by David Toms, the 2001 USPGA champion.

about a foot, he added another at the 14th, and then played the 18th with a two iron and five iron inside 18 feet, his fourth birdie of the day.

Speaking later, Waldorf claimed he missed quite a few iron shots, "but I was missing them straight," which certainly helped.

By the time Toms teed off, at 1.35, Muirfield was playing faster than it had in the morning, and Toms took advantage. He did come into the championship with some confidence. After all, he was the last man to win one of the game's major championships that Woods didn't, and he could drive the ball quite long for an average-sized man and at the same time keep it in play.

Grouped with the Irishman Darren Clarke and the American Kevin Sutherland, Toms played quite a steady round. With birdies on both the third and fourth holes, he went out in 34 and came back in 33, a score that could have been lower. After two more birdies at the 12th and 13th, he lost a stroke on the 14th, his only bogey of the day, then picked it up once again at the 17th, a vulnerable par 5.

Two hours later, Pettersson came in with 67 as well, again a score that could have been lower. Wearing a blue shirt, orange cap, blond chin whiskers, and an easy smile, Pettersson said he had never played a links

Players Below Par	37
Players At Par	22
Players Above Par	97

Round of the Day

Carl Pettersson
Game No. 46
Thursday 18 July at 3:30 pm.

ROUND 1

Hole	1	2	3	4	5	6	7	8	9	Out
Yards	448	351	378	213	560	468	185	443	508	3554
Par	4	4	4	3	5	4	3	4	5	36
Score	4	4	3	3	4	4	3	4	4	33

Signature of Marker

10	11	12	13	14	15	16	17	18	In	Total
475	389	381	191	448	415	186	546	449	3480	7034
4	4	4	3	4	4	3	5	4	35	71
4	3	4	3	5	3	3	4	5	34	67

Signature of Competitor

Carl Pettersson was the only one to reach five under par in the first round when he made his sixth birdie of the day on the 17th hole. The 24-year-old Swede, who lives in Raleigh, North Carolina, then took a bogey 5 on the 18th to finish with 67, four under par,

and have a share of the opening day lead.

In his second year on the PGA European Tour, Pettersson was playing in his first Open Championship. "I only missed two fairways, the first and the 18th," Pettersson said. "I had good opportunities all the way round and I had a few putts going in. I

started the round by making a 20-footer for par and that was a nice way to get me jump-started.

"The pins were tricky and the first par 3 was really tough. I was above the hole there. I made a great two-putt for par. There were a few other tricky ones if you got on the wrong side of the hole."

course until this week, yet his lack of exposure to this kind of golf didn't seem to bother him.

The son of an executive with Volvo Trucks, Pettersson was born in Sweden, but when his father was transferred, he lived in England from the age of 10 until he reached 15, then moved to North Carolina, and played golf for North Carolina State University.

He still kept ties to Europe, and in 2000 won the European Amateur Championship. Joining the PGA European Tour the following year, he placed second in the Argentine Open, and earlier in 2002 won the Algarve Open de Portugal.

While this was his first Open, when he birdied the 17th hole, he became the only man to go five under par. He had gone out in 33 with birdies on the third, fifth, and ninth, and reached the 17th tee four under par. There he birdied once again, dipping five under, but he lost a stroke on the home hole and fell back to 67.

Carl Pettersson had an Open debut to remember.

It's a
Fact

A score of 66 is the best ever recorded by a competitor in the opening round of his first appearance in the Open Championship. It was done first by John Schroeder at Turnberry in 1977, then by Wayne Stephens at Royal Troon in 1989, by Lee Janzen at Muirfield in 1992, and by Jonathan Lomas at Turnberry in 1994.

Is It Justin's Time?

On the Thursday of the Open Justin Rose came downstairs for breakfast and immediately Ken, his father, saw something he liked. His son, Ken noted, was calm and collected, demonstrating poise. On the morning of the day when Justin would play his first round with Tiger Woods, the 21-year-old demonstrated that he was not going to be overawed.

"I could see in his eyes that he was going to be okay," Ken Rose said. "He looked so relaxed. He had a really good attitude. I noticed that he was so positive right from when I first saw him. We had a really good discussion, too. I said to him, 'Jus, don't forget your bubble of concentration. Tiger will be in his, you stay in yours.'"

And so it proved. Rose went round in 68, three under par and one stroke behind the leaders, two strokes ahead of Woods. There was no doubt it had been his day more than it had been Tiger's. When was the last time Woods was outscored by both his playing partners and when was the last major championship in which Woods was outscored by a man five years younger? The answers would seem to be: not recently and never against the world No 1.

Earlier in the week, when it became known that Rose, who had won four tournaments on three continents in the year to date, was to be paired with Woods, an air of excitement spread around Muirfield. "It is going to be harder in terms of everything else going on around the golf—bigger crowds, more noise—but it also makes it more fun," Rose said. "It is something I want to do. I want to compete against Tiger sooner rather than later and I've got to play with him for the first time at some stage, so to do it in the Open Championship in front of British fans, there is no better place."

Rose played steady, controlled golf from the moment he hit a two iron that split the narrow first fairway. He followed this with

birdies on the second and third holes and an eagle on the ninth. Rose looked in control of himself. He did not get ahead of himself. All those missed cuts he had endured after turning professional almost exactly four years earlier had taught him something—and today was the day he demonstrated just what that was.

—*John Hopkins*

Justin Rose was well served by two irons off the tees.

With so little experience in championship golf, it didn't seem likely Pettersson would threaten at the end. At the same time, much of the gallery held high hopes for Justin Rose, even though at 21 he was three years younger than Pettersson.

Rose, though, had been around longer. He first drew attention when, as a 17-year-old schoolboy, he played well enough at Royal Birkdale to tie for fourth in the 1998 Open, then immediately turned to professional golf.

It seemed a foolish decision at the time, especially when he missed the 36-hole cut in 21 consecutive tournaments, but Rose persevered. He had to go through three sessions of qualifying, then finally tasted some success during 2001, where he placed 33rd in the Order of Merit.

Before coming to Muirfield, Rose had won four tournaments in 2002 and placed among the top 10 finishers in six. Even so, when he stepped onto the first tee along with Tiger Woods, he couldn't help feeling a touch nervous.

For his 68, Phil Mickelson birdied the last two holes.

"I think the first time you play with him it's a bit of an eye-opener," Rose said. "There is definitely an aura about him, but I didn't get caught up in all the stuff that goes on around him. I focused on my own game. I realised the Open is an important tournament for me, not just playing with Tiger Woods."

Rose actually played better than Woods this day. Driving mainly with his two iron, he birdied the second with a sand wedge to four feet and the third with an eight iron to 10 feet. Two under par now, he eased through the next five holes in level par, stepped onto the ninth tee, and played two of the best shots of the day.

"There's a horrible little pot bunker about 270 yards out on that hole," Rose said, "so I hit a two iron for safety and got lucky." His ball flew directly at the bunker and somehow pulled up almost at its edge. From there he ripped a four iron 244 yards to the green. The ball hit short, rolled on, took the green's left-to-right cant, and rolled within four feet of the cup.

From the sound of the crowd, Rose thought it might fall for a 2, but it glided past and he holed the putt for an eagle 3 and 32 on the first nine.

In the Words of the Competitors…

"

"The conditions were fantastic and if you were going to go low, today was the day, but no one did that because the course is so tough."

—Paul Lawrie

"One under par through five holes, I had a simple bunker shot, leaving the ball in the bunker. I then bogeyed the next, and so from a very good start I had a very bad start."

—Ernie Els

"I'm 45 years of age and to come here, which to me is the great championship in the world, and to get off to a good start like this, I feel pretty good about it. I feel pretty lucky."

—Mark O'Meara

"What you don't want to do is put yourself out early on. You want to shoot around par or a couple under, that's always good."

—Sergio Garcia

"I took advantage, obviously, of a perfect day in Scotland."

—David Toms

"It's very disappointing because I didn't play well. I got off to a good start with birdies at the second and third and didn't continue."

—Colin Montgomerie

"

Round One Hole Summary

HOLE	PAR	EAGLES	BIRDIES	PARS	BOGEYS	D. BOGEYS	HIGHER	RANK	AVERAGE
1	4	0	7	91	49	9	0	1	4.39
2	4	0	44	106	6	0	0	16	3.76
3	4	0	21	115	20	0	0	13	3.99
4	3	0	9	102	41	4	0	5	3.26
5	5	0	41	85	23	7	0	15	4.97
6	4	0	11	87	50	7	1	2	4.37
7	3	0	13	121	19	3	0	10	3.08
8	4	0	8	98	46	4	0	4	4.30
9	5	4	90	51	10	1	0	18	4.45
OUT	**36**	**4**	**244**	**856**	**264**	**35**	**1**		**36.55**
10	4	0	7	95	49	4	1	3	4.34
11	4	0	30	99	23	4	0	12	4.01
12	4	0	18	125	11	2	0	14	3.98
13	3	0	21	100	33	2	0	9	3.10
14	4	0	13	94	45	4	0	5	4.26
15	4	0	19	109	26	2	0	11	4.07
16	3	0	9	104	39	4	0	7	3.24
17	5	2	62	73	15	1	3	17	4.74
18	4	0	16	97	38	4	1	8	4.21
IN	**35**	**2**	**195**	**896**	**279**	**27**	**5**		**35.96**
TOTAL	**71**	**6**	**439**	**1752**	**543**	**62**	**6**		**72.51**

American Steve Jones, with 68, was back on form.

Suddenly his game left him. He gained no more ground on the homeward nine, and came back in 36, one over par. Still, he stood among the leaders, which Colin Montgomerie couldn't say.

After following an opening par with a pair of birdies, Montgomerie played loose golf. By the time he reached the ninth he had gone from two under par to one over, courtesy of a double bogey 6 on the eighth, but he birdied there and finished the first nine at level par. Still level par going to the 14th, he hacked his ball from the rough into a pot bunker and took another 6 on a par-4 hole.

Two over now, Montgomerie bogeyed the 18th as well and stepped off the final green with 74 and nerve ends jangling over the reality that if he played another round like that, he wouldn't survive the 36-hole cut.

Jose Maria Olazabal (above) dropped two shots over the last five holes for 73, while Americans Bob Estes (right) and Davis Love III (below) were in with 71.

"Padraig Harrington is an Irishman, a real Dubliner, but you don't hear anyone making Irish jokes about him. He is far too serious, meticulous and thoughtful for that, certainly when it comes to his golf."

—**Patricia Davies**, *The Times*

"Will this, one wonders, be the year of the Scandinavians? There have been five winners from Denmark and Sweden on the European Tour this season and the great Dane himself, Bjorn, is there among the 68s."

—**Brian Meek**, *The Herald*

"Sandy Lyle's renaissance continued in the Open at Muirfield yesterday. Three months ago it was feared that at 44, he was, like Seve Ballesteros, the victim of competitive burn-out. But there has been a jauntiness in his step in recent weeks, … and Lyle quietly returned to the sort of round that had the juices flowing freely again."

—**Jock McVicar**, *Daily Express*

"David Toms is the last guy besides Tiger Woods to win a major in the last 12 months, which must count for something."

—**Mike Kern**, *Philadelphia Daily News*

A Wave of Low Scores

By Robert Sommers

When he left Thursday evening, Colin Montgomerie felt dejected by his ragged opening round. With a score of 74, three over Muirfield's par, it seemed likely he would have to shoot in the 60s Friday to survive for the weekend. And he showed no confidence he could do it.

"I'll try to rally, of course," Montgomerie said. "I came here full of expectation, but it was no good. It will be very difficult now."

To the contrary, it was easy.

Playing the game his army of supporters felt sure he could, Montgomerie swept round Muirfield in 64 strokes, set the course record, and leapt from a tie for 106th place into a tie for ninth.

Monty wasn't alone in having his way with this storied old course, for this was a day of exceptionally low scoring. Of the 153 men who finished the second round, 69 either broke or matched par—about 45 percent of the field. The course gave up 39 rounds in the 60s, 19 of 70, and 11 more of 71.

Ernie Els raced through the first nine in 29 strokes, one stroke off the championship record, shot 66, and jumped to the top of the standings, tied at 136 with Shigeki Maruyama, Padraig Harrington, Duffy Waldorf, and Bob Tway. The 1986 USPGA champion, Tway had been relatively quiet since he birdied from a bunker on the final hole and snatched the USPGA from Greg Norman, but he, Mark Calcavecchia, the 1989 Open champion, and the Frenchman Thomas Levet all shot 66s as well.

With Muirfield yielding so many sub-70 scores, the field had become so tightly bunched 16 men stood within two strokes of one another. Other than the five sharing first place, three more had tied for sixth, and eight others tied for ninth.

Carl Pettersson stayed among the leaders with 70, and at 137 shared sixth place with Des Smyth and Denmark's Soren Hansen.

Meantime, Tiger Woods made his move. With an opening 70, he had stood four strokes out of the lead, tied for 23rd place with Els, Tway, and 12 others, but he shot 68 in the second round, and now he sat only two strokes back and behind just eight others. He shared

Shigeki Maruyama wasn't the only one smiling this day.

Excerpts from the
Press

Peter O'Malley's 68 was only his second below-70 round in nine Opens.

"The guys at the front are there to be caught, so why shouldn't I go on to win it?" young Ian Poulter asked.

ninth place with the dangerous Thomas Bjorn, another Dane, Levet, Montgomerie, Nick Price, close friend Mark O'Meara, Stephen Ames, and the young Englishman Ian Poulter.

Price birdied three of the first five holes and fell to six under par, but he lost two strokes over the last 13 and shot 70.

At the same time, David Toms, who had shared the first-round lead at 67, opened with a double bogey 6, went out in 39, shot 75, and dropped to joint 43rd place with 142. Both Steve Jones and Justin Rose shot 75 and at 143 dropped from fourth into a tie for 50th. Phil Mickelson played worse. Driving into Muirfield's impregnable rough, he double-bogeyed the first, double-bogeyed the 14th, shot 76, and, like Sandy Lyle, at 144 barely survived the 36-hole cut.

Showing no spark at all, David Duval added 71 to his first-round 72, and sat close to the bottom of the standings, seven strokes off the lead. Without a surge of spirit, he would not repeat as Open champion.

While the field didn't ravage Muirfield, the rush of low scoring surprised nearly everyone because the conditions had worsened. Unlike Thursday's pleasant weather, an intermittent rain fell much of Friday

before the skies cleared towards late afternoon. The wind had shifted overnight as well, to a northerly breeze, but was still moderate to light.

Darren Clarke felt perplexed.

"Today it's not so nice and the pins are more difficult, and yet the scoring is better," Clarke said. "I'm surprised."

Montgomerie said, "Sometimes when you think you should do something, it doesn't happen. That's golf. We're all expecting Tiger to go round in benign conditions in 66, and it doesn't happen. That's why we're all here. If it was cut and dried we would all go home."

While Montgomerie began his attack on Muirfield at nine o'clock, he had made a critical decision the previous afternoon. Looking into his car he noticed a new set of clubs he'd had the manufacturer make him Tuesday. After Thursday's disappointing round, he thought, "Oh, I'll use these.

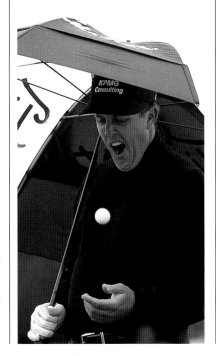

Thomas Bjorn (above) was two off the lead with his 70, despite dropping two shots on the second nine, while Phil Mickelson (left) needed a birdie on the 17th for 76 to make the 36-hole cut.

In the Words of the Competitors...

"

"The most important thing that happened that I can take from today is that I didn't drop a shot. If I can keep doing that, I have a chance here."

—Colin Montgomerie

"I have been in good form for the last few weeks, but to be among the leaders and in the clubhouse after two rounds in the Open is something special, I must say."

—Soren Hansen

"I don't have a jacket that matches the flowered look. It was just too cold for the Californian today."

—Duffy Waldorf

"I have always loved the golf over here. I always wonder when we come over what we did wrong in America about designing golf courses."

—Bob Tway

"I said to the French press it's like a ladder. The first rung is making the cut, then the next is to finish high up, but to go all the way you need a big heart and a bit of luck. It is one step at a time."

—Thomas Levet

"

"They're advertising them on the way to the Open. I saw myself on a big screen as I drove in and said, 'That's me, and I'm using a club I've never used.' So I got them to make me up a set. I didn't use them Thursday, but I used them today."

Montgomerie had played the first hole with a three iron and seven iron Thursday, but with the wind coming directly at him, he rifled a three wood from the tee and followed with a stunning three iron within 20 feet of the hole, ran it in, and was off to one of the great rounds in Muirfield's Open history.

Three routine pars brought him to the fifth, a par 5 of 560 yards. Monty tore into a drive, then ripped a three wood that ran onto the right side of the green, followed the right-to-left slope to the lower level, and pulled up 25 feet from the hole.

The putt dropped for an eagle 3. Three under now, he had wiped out his losses of Thursday and stood at level par for the 21

holes. He wasn't through yet. A drive and a six iron to the tough sixth and another birdie from five feet, then a driver and three wood just off the ninth green, a chip to four feet and still another birdie.

Montgomerie had gone out in 31 strokes and stood five under par for the round, but the tough home nine lay ahead and the birdies didn't come so easily, nor did some of the pars.

His drive at the 11th dived into Muirfield's vicious rough, but he tore the ball out and played a pitch-and-run close enough to salvage par on the 11th. He holed from 30 feet and birdied the 15th, but failed to birdie the 17th, which gave up 60 birdies Friday, the most of any hole. Then he drilled a four iron to 12 feet, birdied the home hole, played the second nine in 33, and stepped off the final green seven under par. He had scored five birdies and an eagle, and yet claimed to be more impressed because he had made no mistakes.

On the 13th green (opposite page) and the eighth tee, the crowds were with Colin Montgomerie's pursuit of a course record.

Round of the Day

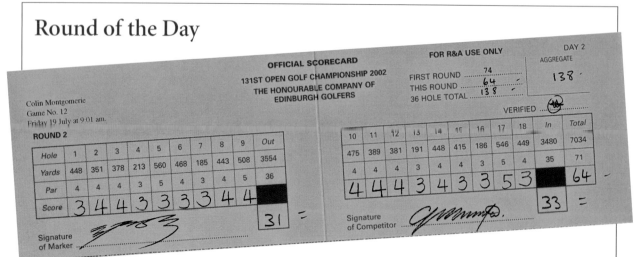

A three iron to 20 feet and a birdie 3 on the first hole set Colin Montgomerie off towards a score of 64, seven under par, in a round without a single bogey. "It's one of those unexplainable things," Montgomerie said. "That is the beauty of golf, that you can score a very poor 74 yesterday and a good 64 today."

Montgomerie went out in 31 with a three wood to 25 feet for an eagle 3 on the fifth, a six iron to five feet for a birdie 3 on the sixth, and a chip to four feet for a birdie 4 at the ninth. He birdied the 15th from 30 feet and the 18th with a four iron to 12 feet.

"I want to keep this momentum going," Montgomerie said. "I know I can win. I have never been frightened of winning. I think my last hole proved that. I've just got to use that psychology, if you like, in a positive way, over the weekend."

Replicas of the trophy and belt were on display.

"Forget the birdies and eagles," Montgomerie said. "It was the lack of bogeys that was important today."

By setting the course record, Montgomerie took his place among some of the greatest names in golf. Walter Hagen had set the Muirfield record at 67 in the second round in 1929, when he won his fourth Open. Henry Cotton lowered it to 66 in 1948, and then Peter Butler shot 65 in 1966, although Jack Nicklaus won. Isao Aoki shot 63, the lowest score ever, in 1980, the year Tom Watson won his third Open.

Alterations to the course, however, meant that Montgomerie's 64 stood as the new record, even though Aoki had done better and Watson, Hubert Green, Horacio Carbonetti, Rodger Davis, Steve Pate, Raymond Floyd, and Nick Faldo all had shot 64s before him.

All that mattered not at all at this stage of

Up and Down With Monty

By Andy Farrell

If ever a round of golf was inspired by pure strength of will, a deep personal craving for justification, even perhaps a hint of desperation, it was the 64 scored by Colin Montgomerie in the second round. It took Montgomerie from three over par, where the threat of missing the cut was very real, to four under par, and into contention towards the top of the leaderboard.

It was deemed a new course record for Muirfield, although the 63 of Isao Aoki, compiled in the third round of the 1980 Open, remains the lowest score ever recorded at the magnificent East Lothian links. The course was extended by around 60 yards for this year's championship, so the lowest round of the week, which Monty's effort remained, became the new official record.

On this dank, heavy morning when light rain was in the air but the breeze steadfastly refused to get up, Montgomerie produced a succession of brilliant iron shots and capitalised on his fine approach play by holing a number of important putts. It perhaps goes without saying that such a round at Muirfield can be compiled no other way.

But Montgomerie's cannot be divorced from the wider context of the championship and the Scot's roller coaster of the season. Just the previous day, Monty had scored 74. Although he would outdo himself in the differential department later in the championship, an improvement of 10 strokes between late Thursday evening and early Friday morning was its own little masterpiece.

Little had gone right on Thursday, but the end of his round particularly disappointed Montgomerie. He failed to birdie the 17th and then bogeyed the 18th. The 5 at the last was caused by a tee shot that failed to make the fairway.

"It was 207 yards to clear the rough and I didn't do it," he said. "It was a disappointing shot. It was a disappointing round. I had a big think."

Room service was the order of the evening back at his hotel, and he decided to switch his irons to a set that had only been made up earlier in the week. Immediately he felt a difference, although the quality of his long game was most helped by properly completing the backswing, something that is probably dependent on the day-to-day state of his aching back.

"Forget the birdies, the key today was that there were no bogeys," Montgomerie said. "I couldn't afford to drop a shot. I was fortunate to be playing late-early, because I didn't have 24 hours to dwell on it and read your newspapers."

This last comment was a reference to Montgomerie's often turbulent relationship with certain sections of the press. But nothing any journalist had written could have as much affect on Montgomerie's psyche as his own intense desire to succeed.

"There is only one person that is affected by anything. The 74 was so disappointing yesterday I wanted to go out and prove to one person I can do this. There is nobody here," Montgomerie said as he looked out over a packed interview room, "with all respect to you all, that I wanted to prove it to. I wanted to prove to myself that I can still do this, still compete at this level, and I did that today."

For a decade during which he won seven successive European Order of Merits, a record that may stand the test of time, Montgomerie was the most consistent player on tour. Recently, not helped by a worrying back condition, he had become one of the most inconsistent. His season contained more ups and downs than the financial markets.

At the Scottish Open at Loch Lomond the week before the Open, he was despondent about his game for three days, then had never played better in the final round.

Montgomerie had only broken 70 once in his previous 16 rounds in the Open, a 65 in the first round last year. The Scot led for each of the first two days at Royal Lytham but faded over the weekend. As well as having on his bag Andy Prodger, Nick Faldo's caddie at Muirfield in 1987, Monty's putting had improved on a year previously thanks to a putter that he anchors in his stomach.

"Leading the Open for that length of time is a difficult task. Coming from behind, shooting a 64 on Friday, was a lot easier," he said.

After a contretemps with a radio reporter on Thursday evening, at lunchtime the next day, after fulfilling all his media obligations, Montgomerie said, "Peace has broken out." It was a brief ceasefire.

Pettersson's Unusual Route to Success

The first question was, "Who?" And the answer was Carl Pettersson. After having 67 to be among the leaders in the first round, Pettersson did not post a high number in the second round, as might have been expected of a player in his first Open Championship. He followed with a solid one-under-par 70 and was one stroke off the lead through 36 holes. The Open has had its share of surprises, but you would have to go back a long way to find one with a resume as unlikely as this one.

Pettersson, 24 years of age, was born in Sweden and moved to North Carolina at 15 when his father was sent to the United States by his company. He stayed when his family moved back several years ago.

He played on the golf team at North Carolina State University, but cost his team a crack at the American collegiate championship with an incorrect scorecard in a regional qualifying event. He still lives in Raleigh, but plays on the PGA European Tour. He ranked 61st in earnings in 2001, his first year, and achieved his first victory in the 2002 Algarve Open de Portugal.

Being just one stroke off the lead at the halfway point was not bad for a guy whose driver wasn't on speaking terms with Muirfield's fairways, which demand accuracy more than distance.

"I hit three drivers today," Pettersson said. "I have a pretty low ball flight, so I can keep it under the wind. I've hit a lot of two irons, which have been working."

Pettersson kept his game under tight rein. He got to two under par in a hurry. He birdied the second hole with a three iron and a wedge to two feet, then the par-5 fifth, where he hit a driver and a three wood, and got down in two from a bunker. He had only one bogey—and two in the first round when he missed the green at the par-3 seventh. He marched in from there with 11 consecutive pars.

Pettersson took up golf at the age of 10, after having, as he put it, "messed around" with the game as a toddler near his birthplace, Gothenburg. He got help from his father, Lars, a low handicapper, who took his family to America when his company, Volvo Trucks, transferred him. It turned out to be a career move for Carl.

"I think it improved my game tremendously, being able to practice in good weather nearly all year round," he said. Then there was the competitive American Junior Golf Association, and then collegiate golf. So, at the Open, Pettersson was hardly a timid soul.

"It feels great," Pettersson said. "I know there's a long way to go, but I'm excited about the weekend and pleased with the way I'm playing right now."

—*Marino Parascenzo*

Nick Price had three bogeys, but was only two strokes back.

the Open. Montgomerie had nearly finished when Els teed off shortly after one o'clock, about 40 minutes ahead of Woods. Since he first established himself as a powerful force in the game, Woods had had an intimidating effect on Els. Two years earlier at St Andrews, Ernie had asked, "How are you going to beat this guy?"

Before the 2002 championship opened, someone asked Els about criticism he had heard that he, David Duval, and Phil Mickelson hadn't given Woods enough of a challenge.

"When I'm playing well," Els responded, "I feel I have a chance to win. When I've played well, Tiger has still beaten me. What do you do?"

For his 66, Ernie Els played two over on the second nine.

Low Scores

Low First Nine
Ernie Els   29

Low Second Nine
Warren Bennett   31

Low Round
Colin Montgomerie   64

Second Round Leaders

HOLE	1	2	3	4	5	6	7	8	9	10	11	12	13	14	15	16	17	18	
PAR	4	4	4	3	5	4	3	4	5	4	4	4	3	4	4	3	5	4	TOTAL
Ernie Els	(3)	(3)	(3)	3	(4)	(3)	3	(3)	(4)	4	[5]	4	[4]	4	4	3	5	4	66-136
Shigeki Maruyama	[5]	(3)	4	3	5	4	3	4	(4)	(3)	4	4	3	4	4	3	(4)	4	68-136
Padraig Harrington	4	(3)	(3)	(2)	5	4	3	[5]	(4)	[5]	(3)	4	3	4	4	3	(4)	4	67-136
Duffy Waldorf	4	4	[5]	3	5	4	[4]	4	(3)	[5]	4	(3)	3	4	(3)	3	(4)	4	69-136
Bob Tway	4	4	(3)	(2)	(4)	[5]	3	4	(4)	4	(3)	4	3	4	4	3	(4)	4	66-136
Soren Hansen	4	4	4	3	(4)	4	3	4	5	4	4	4	3	4	4	3	(4)	4	69-137
Carl Pettersson	4	(3)	4	3	(4)	4	[4]	4	5	4	4	4	3	4	4	3	5	4	70-137
Des Smyth	4	4	4	3	(4)	4	(2)	4	(4)	4	[5]	4	3	4	4	3	5	4	69-137
Colin Montgomerie	(3)	4	4	3	(3)	(3)	3	4	(4)	4	4	4	3	4	(3)	3	5	(3)	64-138
Nick Price	(3)	(3)	4	3	(4)	4	3	[5]	5	[5]	(3)	4	[4]	4	4	3	5	4	70-138
Stephen Ames	4	4	4	3	(3)	4	(2)	[5]	5	[5]	(3)	4	3	[5]	4	3	5	4	70-138
Thomas Levet	(3)	(3)	4	3	5	(3)	3	4	5	4	4	4	3	(3)	4	3	(4)	4	66-138
Mark O'Meara	4	4	(3)	3	5	4	3	4	5	4	4	4	3	4	(3)	3	5	(3)	69-138
Tiger Woods	4	4	(3)	3	(4)	4	3	4	5	4	4	4	3	4	4	3	(4)	4	68-138
Thomas Bjorn	4	4	4	3	(4)	(3)	(2)	4	5	[5]	[5]	4	3	4	(3)	3	5	[5]	70-138
Ian Poulter	[5]	(3)	4	3	5	4	(2)	4	(4)	4	4	4	3	4	4	3	5	4	69-138

Thomas Levet's 66 had five birdies, no bogeys.

Later Els said, "I work hard at my game. When I've had it going, I still got beat. Maybe I'm not good enough."

Els certainly played well enough through the first nine to beat anybody. He began with four consecutive 3s, three for birdies. Even though the first hole played into the wind, Els reached it with a two iron and a four iron that settled within perhaps 12 feet. He followed with a four iron and sand wedge to 15 feet on the second, then a two iron and sand wedge to eight feet on the third.

Pulling out his driver for the first time, Ernie found the fifth fairway, then laid a four iron just short of the green, rolled the ball to 12 feet, and holed for still another birdie. Four under now, he ran into trouble on the sixth. His three wood flew off line into deep grass, and he did well to rip the ball free, although short of the green. No problem; he chipped in from 55 feet, his fifth birdie in six holes.

Another fine pitch to the eighth braked inside five feet, and Els reached the ninth with his second shot and two-putted for an outgoing 29. He had played the first nine with seven 3s and only two 4s, both for birdies. He had shot 70 in the first round, and now he stood eight under par for 27 holes.

His great run had ended, though. Distracted on the 10th tee,

Soren Hansen (top left) shot 69 without a bogey, and was one stroke behind, while Duffy Waldorf (top right) and Padraig Harrington (left) were among the leaders despite combining for five bogeys.

In the Words of the Competitors...

"

"Today was just one of those days I had to stay as patient as possible."

—Tiger Woods

"I'm going to have to start hitting the ball better if I want a chance to win this championship, because the kind of ball striking I had today catches up with you. I have to sort something out. It wasn't pretty."

—Nick Price

"Obviously the eagle on the ninth was a bonus. I was just trying to get it close and it went in (from 40 feet)."

—Retief Goosen

If you keep that going you could shoot 58. That in itself is a scary thought. I didn't quite play to the same level on the second nine.

—Ernie Els

"It's tough work but I am enjoying it. In some sick sense I actually like it."

—Padraig Harrington

"When my first drive of the round went right and I made a double bogey, I knew I was in for a tough day."

—Phil Mickelson

"

he stepped away from his ball, then drove into the rough. While he salvaged a par 4, something had gone from his game. He missed fairways, missed greens, and holed nothing. He overshot the 11th green, chipped back to six feet, mis-read the putt, and bogeyed. Caught in a greenside bunker at the 13th, he took two strokes to escape and holed a nervous five-footer to save a bogey.

Two of his strokes gone, Els came back in 37, shot his 66, and climbed into first place at 136, six under par for 36 holes.

When Els finished, Maruyama, Harrington, Waldorf, and Tway still had holes to play. Grouped with Woods, Maruyama survived a rocky start, driving into the rough on the first, the only fairway he missed all day, and losing a stroke. Quickly, though, he holed from inside 10 feet on the second and scored a two-putt birdie on the ninth. Out in 35, he

Tiger Woods saved par whenever needed.

birdied the 10th by holing from 45 feet, and added another at the 17th, getting down in two from what must have been 70 feet or more.

Maruyama had played beautifully. Besides missing only one fairway, he hit 15 greens, scrambled for his pars on the fourth and 15th, and birdied four holes. Equally important, in two rounds he had given up only two bogeys, dropping shots on the 14th in the first round and the first in the second.

With better luck, Woods would have beaten Maruyama's score, even though he didn't play as well. Despite driving with iron clubs, hoping to avoid trouble, he caught the rough on both the first and second holes, yet still saved his pars. A wedge to four feet set up a birdie on the third, and after another putt slipped past the hole of the fourth, Woods hit a wild drive on the fifth, the sort that ruined his week at Royal Lytham & St Annes in 2001.

As caddies, players, and marshals bellowed,

Maruyama narrowly missed his putt for eagle 3 on the 17th from the back fringe.

One stroke off the lead after his 69, Des Smyth said he "really worked hard today."

Players Below Par	**58**
Players At Par	**11**
Players Above Par	**86**

"Fore right," his ball soared so far off line it carried over the deepest rough, past the gallery ropes, and beyond the spectators. He had struck the ball so badly he found it playable, lying on grass tramped flat by the galleries, another example of the luck that drives rivals mad.

From a decent lie, Woods rifled a two iron 230 yards just short of the green. No one could say this shot resulted from anything other than control of the clubhead and absolute confidence in his swing.

From his position, the green tilts gently towards the hole before crossing a ridge, then slopes down to a lower level. More than one man had played from a similar position, but they had all misjudged the break, either allowing too much or not enough. Woods played it just right. Putting from six or eight feet off the green, he rolled his ball down the slight grade, watched it take the break, turn left, and barely miss an eagle 3. He had no more than a little tap-in for the birdie 4.

Missing another birdie opportunity from five feet on the ninth, Woods went out in 34, two under par, and started back by missing the 10th fairway and green. A 12-footer dropped and he saved the par 4. Just short of the 14th green, he saved another par, and scored his only birdie of the

Paradox of the First Two Rounds

By the end of Friday's second round, a paradox had become apparent, and Padraig Harrington was only one player who highlighted it. How had he been able to go round in 67, four under par, when the weather was wet and unpleasant, whereas on the previous day, when the weather had been benign and ideal for scoring, he had gone round in 69? Harrington was not alone in scoring better in the second round than he had in the first. Colin Montgomerie had a 64 that was 10 strokes better than his first round, and Ernie Els, who went round in 66, in which he went to the turn in 29, compared with 70 the previous day, did the same.

Harrington said he thought that his round represented a release of tension that had unexpectedly built up the day before. "I went out in the first round, as with any major championship, just trying to stay there and not make too many mistakes, to give myself an opportunity," the Irishman said. "I did not want to blow myself out of the tournament straight away. So I played very conservatively early on. I even hit a five iron off the ninth tee."

On Friday Harrington realised that the best form of defence can sometimes be to attack. Perhaps he, and many others, knew that if they did not attack the course, then someone else would and they would be forced to play a form of catch-up golf, which they did not want.

Harrington birdied the second, third, and fourth holes, his longest putt being one of 12 feet on the second. He bogeyed the eighth and 10th, and birdied the ninth and 11th, holing on the 11th from 20 feet. He reached the 17th with a three wood from the tee and another three wood from the fairway and got his sixth birdie for his 67 that took him into a share of the lead with Els, Shigeki Maruyama, Duffy Waldorf, and Bob Tway.

Harrington, one of the most improved players in world golf, had been in a similar position to this in the two previous major championships. At the Masters he led after 27 holes, and at the US Open he had been in the last group playing with Tiger Woods in the third round. It was time he took advantage of it. "There is a lot of work to be done," he said. "But it has to help that I have been there before. With experience you get better and better at it. Whether I will be able to do it this weekend, who knows, but at least I'm in a position to keep trying."

—John Hopkins

---

home nine on the 17th, even though he flew his second shot into the rough and still didn't reach the green with his third.

Speaking of his frustrating day with the putter, Woods said later, "I told myself that if I can't make a putt on the green, then I'll make one from off the green. Lo and behold, that's what happened."

He might have finished a few strokes lower, but putts grazed the holes of the 13th and 15th and spun out on the 16th. Nevertheless, he had let the field know he was still in the chase.

Woods, of course, had been expected to challenge for the championship. On the other hand, Tway and Smyth ranked as total surprises. Smyth even considered himself lucky to have started. Arriving from Geneva Monday, he had rented a car and driven to Muirfield from Edinburgh. Too tired to play more than nine holes, he putted a little, then climbed into his car to

Stephen Ames was elated at the 16th with his par 3.

Round Two Hole Summary

HOLE	PAR	EAGLES	BIRDIES	PARS	BOGEYS	D. BOGEYS	HIGHER	RANK	AVERAGE
1	4	0	12	79	55	9	0	1	4.39
2	4	0	34	98	21	2	0	13	3.94
3	4	0	35	109	11	0	0	14	0.05
4	3	0	14	110	26	4	1	7	3.15
5	5	9	51	76	16	2	1	17	4.71
6	4	0	21	77	45	11	1	2	4.32
7	3	0	22	105	25	2	1	12	3.07
8	4	0	19	105	30	1	0	11	4.08
9	5	4	56	78	12	3	2	16	4.74
OUT	36	13	264	837	241	34	6		36.26
10	4	0	11	102	35	6	1	4	4.25
11	4	0	41	98	15	1	0	14	3.85
12	4	0	16	105	31	3	0	9	4.14
13	3	0	13	113	24	4	1	8	3.14
14	4	0	12	97	40	5	1	3	4.27
15	4	0	21	97	30	5	2	6	4.16
16	3	0	11	117	26	1	0	10	3.11
17	5	3	60	78	12	2	0	18	4.68
18	4	0	15	101	31	8	0	5	4.21
IN	35	3	200	908	244	35	5		35.79
TOTAL	71	16	464	1745	485	69	11		72.05

Being from Oklahoma, where the wind blows, Bob Tway always thought he should play well in the Open.

wait for a friend. Tilting the seat back, he slung one foot over the steering wheel, the other onto the dashboard, and fell asleep for about 15 minutes. He woke with a stiff back that felt worse Tuesday morning.

Physical therapists told Smyth he had put pressure on a nerve and that he shouldn't play. He skipped a practice round Wednesday, but he went out Thursday and shot 68, then followed with 69 Friday. With 137 for 36 holes, he had tied for sixth place, one stroke off the lead.

Still, at 49 years of age, he held no illusions.

"I'm in for the weekend," Smyth

As a past US Open champion, Retief Goosen had "more belief in myself."

said. "My next ambition is to stay among the top 15 and get an exemption for next year. Anything else is a bonus."

Among the late starters, Tway had only one blemish in his round, a bogey 5 on the sixth, where he was bunkered. The bogey ended a string of three straight birdies, but he made up for it by reaching the ninth green with two three woods, then two-putted for his fourth birdie. Out in 33, he came back in 33 as well, picking up birdies on the 11th and 17th, and with 66 took a share of first place.

Perhaps even more important to Tway, he had made the cut, something he had not done at the Open since 1991 at Royal Birkdale, where he tied for fifth behind Ian Baker-Finch.

Many others didn't. The cut fell at 144, two over par, and caught Jose Maria Olazabal, the winner of two Masters Tournaments, along with Michael Campbell, who finished one stroke behind John Daly and Costantino Rocca at St Andrews in 1995; Alex Cejka, among the early leaders at Lytham in 2001; Tom Lehman, the 1996 champion; Billy Mayfair, who tied Nick Faldo for fifth place in the US Open a month earlier; John Cook, second to Faldo at Muirfield in 1992; John Daly, the 1995 champion, and, sadly, Tom Watson, the winner of five Open Championships.

Watson had reached the age of 52 in 2002, but the competitive spirit still burned inside him. Grossly disappointed at shooting 149, better than only three others, he said he wasn't sure he would come back at Royal St George's in 2003. That, however, was a long time off, and time often heals wounds of the spirit. The Open would be the poorer without him.

"The dictatorship of Tiger Woods came under fierce attack yesterday from men he has trodden so deep into golf's fairways they exist on a diet of his divots. This was the day the downtrodden finally rose up and yelled they had had enough of labouring in the shadow of the master."

—**Oliver Holt**, *Daily Mirror*

"Muirfield, as only a classic Scottish links can, delivered more great stuff on Friday in the second round, producing sweeping haymakers amid a steady drizzle, leaving the Open primed for a can't-miss weekend."

—**Brian Murphy,**
San Francisco Chronicle

"It was as if the established names in British and Irish golf woke up yesterday and collectively decided that they had read rather enough, thank you very much, about Justin Rose."

—**Derek Lawrenson**, *Daily Mail*

"Ernie Els was upset to read recent criticism from several aging past champions who questioned why none of the game's current stars was elevating his game to challenge No 1 Tiger Woods. This afternoon, under slate-gray spitting skies on a rain-softened links, Els took matters into his own capable hands."

—**Leonard Shapiro,**
Washington Post

Third Round

A Miserable Day for Most

By Robert Sommers

Early Saturday morning, Justin Leonard and Justin Rose played Muirfield in 68 strokes each, an improvement over their respective rounds of 72 and 75 Friday, but when they finished they stood in 27th place, hopelessly out of the chase. The round over, Rose wandered to the clubhouse and Leonard putted for a while, then left for his room in Greywalls, the hotel alongside Muirfield's ninth hole.

The longer they sat, the higher they climbed in the standings. When they struck their first shots shortly after 10 o'clock, they foundered in 50th place. By day's end, they had climbed within three strokes of first, tied for third at 211 behind Ernie Els at 208 and Dane Soren Hansen at 210. The great men who had begun the day so far ahead of them had fallen on their swords.

Ernie Els finished strongly with par here at the 15th, two birdies and a final par.

Battered by wind and rain, and playing in frigid temperatures, the late starters struggled through a miserable day, one of the worst within memory. The wind swept in from the north at a steady 25 miles an hour with gusts much stronger. It drove the rain sideways for a while with such force, every drop felt as if it had been shot from a dart gun. Temperatures fell so low, it seemed that the shadowy land mass across the water was not the east neuk of Fife, as spectators had been told, but, rather, the North Pole.

The game's best golfers couldn't control their shots; anything that settled within sight of a green drew applause. If this had been anything other than the Open Championship, half the field might have withdrawn and gone home. Maybe the players couldn't, but the crowd could and did. When the rain poured down at its worst, spectators who had swarmed through the gates in early morning streamed back out again, leaving the huge grandstands almost empty.

Players' hands became so cold they had trouble gripping a club. Hacking his way through the rough, Nick Faldo double-bogeyed the sixth and went out in 39. Phil Mickelson hit only two of the first seven fairways and four of the first nine greens and matched

As Sergio Garcia teed off on the sixth, the approaching storm was visible behind him.

Faldo's 39. Then, not playing like the seasoned professional which he was, David Toms, the 2001 USPGA champion, played the sixth, seventh, and eighth in 6, 3, 8, six over par. He shot 81 and dropped into a tie for last place with Lee Janzen, twice the US Open champion, who went out in 43 with a birdie on the ninth and shot 84.

Where the 560-yard fifth hole had been reached routinely with the second shot, playing into the wind it couldn't always be reached with the third. Even the fourth hole, a 213-yard par 3, reachable with perhaps a five iron in normal weather, demanded the heavy artillery. Seeing Colin Montgomerie's three wood fall short, Nick Price played his driver and barely made the green.

"That's normally my 270- to 280-yard club," Price said. "I hit it maybe 208 yards."

It was a perfect day to huddle by the fireside with a warm toddy and remember there had been worse days at the Open.

Rain had struck Royal Birkdale in 1998, bringing wind that blustered so strongly balls wouldn't stay put on the greens, which caused Royal and Ancient officials to discontinue play temporarily. When Arnold Palmer

From being draped in national colours, competitors and spectators switched to rain gear and umbrellas.

"Whipping winds raged off the Firth of Forth, spewing cold rain that sent Tiger Woods to his worst round as a professional—an 81!—and swept away his chances of winning all four majors in the same year."

—**Doug Ferguson,**
The Associated Press

"Despite all the experience of links golf at Clarke's home course of Portmarnoch, he was still blown away in the most brutal conditions to hit an Open Championship in years."

—**Ken Lawrence,** *Sunday Mirror*

"Thomas Bjorn and Soren Hansen of Denmark and Carl Pettersson, the burly Swede, put on their cold-weather masks and battled through the storm."

—**Eddie Butler,** *The Observer*

"Tiger Woods has one more thing in common with Jack Nicklaus. It appears that both of them have lost a Grand Slam opportunity at Muirfield."

—**Glenn Sheeley,**
Atlanta Journal-Constitution

"As the wind picked up, the tent poles began to creak and the drizzle degenerated into a downpour, the young Englishman (Rose) scuttled off into the clubhouse hoping that doom-laden forecasts would work in his favour."

—**Paul Forsyth,** *Scotland on Sunday*

brought renewed attention to the Open by entering in 1960, rain fell so heavily on the Old Course, the traditional double round had to be abandoned and the fourth round postponed until the next day. A year later gales roared across Royal Birkdale leveling just about everything but the huge exhibition tent.

The winds were so fierce in 1929 at Muirfield, Henry Longhurst wrote that "Walter Hagen's final rounds of 75 were reckoned some of the finest golf ever played."

Nothing, however, exceeded the carnage of the Great Storm of 1938.

On the evening before the closing double round, a heavy thunderstorm struck and gale force winds swept across Sandwich, ripping the canvas from the huge exhibition tent and scattering merchandise as far as the Prince's clubhouse, three-quarters of a mile off. Steel-shafted clubs lay twisted and broken in the wreckage.

Stuart Appleby was finished with 70 before the last groups were off.

Only the tent poles remained standing, looking, as Longhurst described them, "like a great eight-masted schooner in full sail that a short time ago had sunk with all hands."

Had this been the case at Muirfield in 2002, it would have been safe to say Tiger Woods had gone down with the ship and dragged Montgomerie with him.

Woods shot 81, the worst round he had ever played as a professional, and fresh off setting the course record of 64 on Friday, Montgomerie erupted to 84. Both scores qualified as bizarre.

Thus ended the quest for the Grand Slam. Like Don Quixote, Woods had reached for the unreachable star, and found that this time at least, his arms couldn't stretch high enough.

It should be understood, though, that these were abnormal conditions. Forced to battle through weather that ordinarily would have kept them indoors, golfers wrapped themselves in sweaters and waterproof suits, sheltered behind umbrellas, and did the best they could. For some, it wasn't enough.

Ten men shot in the 80s, and just four shot in the 60s. Close to extinction with 144 over the first 36 holes, both Steve Elkington and Peter Lonard

Round of the Day

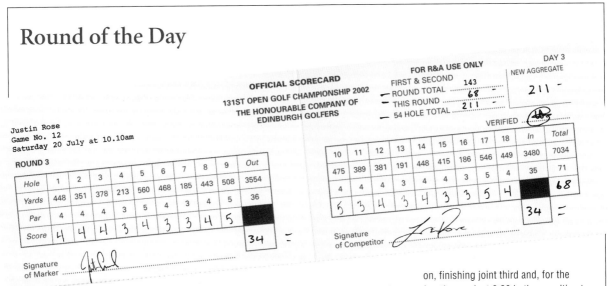

OFFICIAL SCORECARD
131ST OPEN GOLF CHAMPIONSHIP 2002
THE HONOURABLE COMPANY OF
EDINBURGH GOLFERS

FOR R&A USE ONLY
FIRST & SECOND ... 143
— ROUND TOTAL ...... 68 —
— THIS ROUND 211
— 54 HOLE TOTAL ......

DAY 3
NEW AGGREGATE
211 —

VERIFIED ......

Justin Rose
Game No. 12
Saturday 20 July at 10.10am

ROUND 3

Hole	1	2	3	4	5	6	7	8	9	Out
Yards	448	351	378	213	560	468	185	443	508	3554
Par	4	4	4	3	5	4	3	4	5	36
Score	4	4	4	3	4	3	3	4	5	

34 =

Signature of Marker ......

10	11	12	13	14	15	16	17	18	In	Total
475	389	381	191	448	415	186	546	449	3480	7034
4	4	4	3	4	4	3	5	4	35	71
5	3	4	3	4	3	3	5	4		68

34 =

Signature of Competitor ......

Justin Rose was in Game 12 at 10.10 in calm weather, more than five hours before the leaders would play. Rose was paired with another Justin, the 1997 champion Leonard, and both returned 68s, three under par, to place them at 211, two under par for the championship. Just after he finished Rose said, "The wind is picking up and hopefully I have been a bit lucky with the draw."

At the time, their scores did not seem very impressive, because the 36-hole leaders were going off at six under par, but Rose and Leonard steadily progressed as the day went on, finishing joint third and, for the fourth round, at 2.20 in the penultimate Game 41, an improvement of 29 positions.

Three strokes behind, Rose was better off than he could have imagined, as he said earlier, "If the wind were to blow and I was just five shots off the lead at most, then I would be still in with a chance."

matched the 68s of Leonard and Rose, the best scores of the round, and became contenders. Five others shot 70, most notably Stuart Appleby, who would be heard from later, and another nine shot 71. Every one of them had teed off before 10 o'clock, when conditions were more playable.

Like all those near the top after 36 holes, and consequently late starters, Els began at 3.30 and played through some of the worst conditions. But while Scottish weather can be appalling, it is changeable. As Els was playing the second nine of his round, the wind died, the rain stopped, the waterproofs came off, and scoring improved.

Justin Leonard (far left) and Justin Rose had drawn a large crowd by the 14th hole.

Low Scores

Low First Nine

Peter Lonard	32
Jesper Parnevik	32

Low Second Nine

Ernie Els	32
Justin Leonard	32
Duffy Waldorf	32

Low Round

Peter Lonard	68
Steve Elkington	68
Justin Rose	68
Justin Leonard	68

Mark O'Meara shot 77, but that was four strokes better than his pal Tiger.

Scott McCarron (above) was off at 1.35, posting 72 on the cusp of the storm. Peter Lonard (right) returned 68 from his 8.55 start, and Shigeki Maru-yama (far right) had 75 in the final 3.30 group.

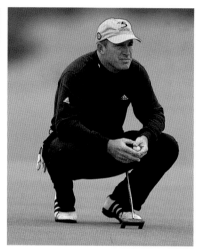

Winds grounded the television balloon, while Thomas Levet played on.

Thomas Bjorn had 73 with four birdies.

Els had stumbled through the first nine in 40, but he came back in 32 and shot 72, the lowest score of those who began after 1.35. One stroke behind the five 36-hole co-leaders, Hansen shot 73 and passed everyone except Els.

Shigeki Maruyama shot 75 and fell into the third-place tie; Padraig Harrington shot 76 and tied for 10th; Duffy Waldorf shot 77 and fell to a tie for 14th; and Bob Tway shot 78 and dropped to a tie for 23rd.

Leonard and Rose, meanwhile, shared third place with Maruyama, Thomas Bjorn, Des Smyth, Scott McCarron, a 37-year-old American playing in only his second Open, and Sergio Garcia, who had been quiet until coming through with 71, one of the better rounds of the day.

With the wind playing tricks, strange happenings became common-place. Waldorf shot 45 on the first nine, yet came back in 32, unreeling a string of five consecutive 3s followed by a 2.

Strangest of all was the collapse of Woods. Over the two years since he had established himself by winning, in succession, the 2000 US Open, the Open Championship, the USPGA, and the 2001 Masters, no one could truly say he had beaten him; others had won when Woods had beaten himself by playing poorly. He had played some awful stuff at Royal Lytham & St Annes in 2001, as well as at Southern Hills in the US Open and at Atlanta Athletic Club in the 2001 USPGA and hadn't threatened to win any of them.

Recovering his form as the 2002 season opened, Woods had been on his game in the Masters and US Open and won them both, and even

Players Below Par	9
Players At Par	9
Players Above Par	65

Steve Elkington birdied two of his last four holes.

Dreams of a Grand Slam
Washed Out, Blown Away

By Ron Sirak

Dawn broke with an eerie calm on Saturday. Only the faintest of breezes ruffled the flags. Tiny shafts of sunlight could be seen between the layer-cake clouds that crossed the Firth of Forth. Truly, it was the calm before the storm. When history pens the final words to the failed Grand Slam bid by Tiger Woods in 2002, it will make large note of the brutal conditions under which he played his third round of the Open Championship.

The day began in the placid eye of the storm and ended that way as well. Those with the earliest of tee times—like Justin Rose and Justin Leonard, who began the day tied for 50th place—and those off at the very end of the day played large parts of their round with a benign breeze.

Woods, however, got the absolute worst of the draw. Teeing off seven groups before the leaders, he played all but two of his holes in the teeth of the storm. Ernie Els, in the last group out, and Duffy Waldorf, in the penultimate group, both capitalised on the passing of the wind and rain and managed 32 on the second nine.

By the time Woods teed off, the rain was starting to blow in horizontal sheets. "It was stinging so hard I kept looking at the ground to see if it was sleet," Woods said. And it did not take long before Woods and his Grand Slam dreams were tossed about like a cork on a high sea. Bogeys on the first and fourth hole were only a prelude to his disaster at the fifth when he made a double bogey 7.

While it is pure speculation, it is perhaps at this point that Woods made his most crucial blunder of the championship. Unlike many of the players with European Tour experience, Woods never seemed to develop the reduced expectations needed to adapt to the conditions. Soren Hansen, Sergio Garcia, Thomas Bjorn, Des Smyth, and Thomas Levet all figured out ways to shoot below 75.

Woods followed his double bogey on No 5 with two more bogeys on the first nine and shot 42 on his way to an 81, by two strokes his highest score ever as a professional. "I tried on each and every shot and that's the best I could have shot," Woods said immediately after the round.

"It was either this or the Australian Open in 1996 (where he posted his previous high of 79) when it was blowing like this, but obviously the golf course wasn't set up like this," Woods said when asked to describe the most difficult conditions in which he had ever played. "It was a tough and frustrating round, but I tried all the way around and it just wasn't meant to be today."

How difficult were the conditions? Woods said he needed a five iron to hit the ball 135 yards on the third hole. "And I hit it good," he added. On the 213-yard fourth hole, Woods's playing companion, Mark O'Meara, hit a driver.

The rain was so constant—Americans are not used to playing in wet weather for that long because if this had been a day in the United States the round would have been stopped by standing water that merely disappeared into the sandy links soil here—that Woods used more than a dozen gloves during the round.

"It was just blowing so hard out there that it was difficult to stand without your body moving," Woods said. "The ball is oscillating, the rain is blowing, and it was just so tough starting out. On top of that, I just hit poor shots and when you add that with the conditions, you are not going to end up with a good result."

There was another obstacle Woods faced on that fateful Saturday. He did not have a hot putter with which to save pars. Even in the first two rounds, when Woods was striking the ball superbly, he was leaving birdie opportunity after birdie opportunity unexploited. While he hit 75 percent of the fairways over the first 36 holes and 81 percent of the greens in regulation, he needed 63 putts in the first two rounds. That ranked him in 114th place in the 153-man field.

On Saturday, when poor weather and sub-par ball striking dropped his fairway accuracy to 50 percent and his greens in regulation to seven of 18 (38.9 percent), Woods still managed only 31 putts. "I was frustrated in a way that I was not able to hit the ball today," he said. "On top of that I didn't make any putts again, so it was just a tough day."

While Woods was a mere mortal in the wind and rain of that round, three-time Open champion Nick Faldo said other players should not take too much hope away from his difficult day.

"Mother Nature beat Tiger," Faldo said. "Not even he can beat the hay here. He'll go away and think about it and he'll be even better equipped next time. It was just a freak of nature. He was probably thinking that if he shoots 61 today (on Sunday) he could still have a chance."

Also brought into sharper focus was the magnitude of the accomplishments by Woods—particularly the four consecutive major championships he won beginning with the 2000 US Open.

Clearly, maybe all those who were conceding a calendar-year sweep of the four major championships to Woods were doing him a disservice by underestimating the enormity of the task. And maybe Jack Nicklaus was right when he said it would be best for golf if Woods completed the same-year slam 10 years from now. Anticipation, after all, is one of the most powerful of human emotions.

Third Round Leaders

HOLE	1	2	3	4	5	6	7	8	9	10	11	12	13	14	15	16	17	18	TOTAL
PAR	4	4	4	3	5	4	3	4	5	4	4	4	3	4	4	3	5	4	TOTAL
Ernie Els	4	[5]	4	[4]	[6]	[5]	3	4	5	4	(3)	4	(2)	[5]	4	(2)	(4)	4	72-208
Soren Hansen	4	[5]	4	3	5	[5]	[4]	4	(4)	4	4	4	3	4	[5]	3	(4)	4	73-210
Justin Leonard	4	4	4	3	5	[5]	3	4	(4)	4	4	(3)	3	(3)	4	3	(4)	4	68-211
Justin Rose	4	4	4	3	(4)	(3)	3	4	5	[5]	(3)	4	3	4	(3)	3	5	4	68-211
Sergio Garcia	(3)	4	4	3	5	4	[4]	4	5	4	4	4	[4]	4	4	3	(4)	4	71-211
Scott McCarron	4	4	[5]	3	5	4	3	4	(4)	[5]	4	4	3	4	4	3	5	4	72-211
Thomas Bjorn	(3)	[5]	4	[5]	(4)	[5]	3	4	5	4	[5]	(3)	[4]	4	4	3	(4)	4	73-211
Des Smyth	[6]	4	4	3	5	4	3	[5]	(4)	4	4	4	3	(3)	4	3	[6]	[5]	74-211
Shigeki Maruyama	(3)	[6]	[5]	3	[7]	[5]	(2)	4	5	[5]	(3)	4	3	4	4	3	5	4	75-211
Steve Elkington	4	(3)	(3)	[4]	(4)	4	3	4	5	4	[5]	4	3	4	(3)	3	(4)	4	68-212
Peter Lonard	4	(3)	(3)	(2)	(3)	[5]	3	(3)	[6]	[5]	4	4	3	4	4	3	5	4	68-212
Thomas Levet	[5]	4	4	[4]	5	[5]	3	4	(4)	[5]	4	4	[4]	(3)	4	3	5	4	74-212
Padraig Harrington	(3)	4	4	[5]	[6]	[5]	[4]	[5]	5	[5]	4	4	[4]	(3)	(3)	3	5	4	76-212

though he had played some mediocre golf through the first two rounds at Muirfield, he had gone into the third round just two strokes behind the 36-hole leaders. And they all knew it.

Woods opened the third round at 2.30, an hour ahead of the final pairing. He drove into the rough, failed to reach the green with his second, and bogeyed. While one lost stroke seemed insignificant at the time, he was off on a wild ride that would ruin his dream of the Grand Slam.

Padraig Harrington vied for the lead early on.

Woods had built his game around sound planning, controlling his shots, avoiding mistakes, and holing putts. Playing through the worst of the day's weather, his plan was useless. Not only could he not control the ball's flight, neither could he control it on the green. The wind constantly threw putts off line—as it did for everyone.

After his opening bogey, Woods appeared to have righted himself, making his figures on the next two holes even though he missed both fairways, but he ran into trouble again on the fourth. Trusting his length, he played an iron from the tee but pushed it into the right rough, where once again he had a good break. Instead of diving into the longest grass, his ball settled on a footpath and he saved a bogey 4.

For the second consecutive year, the luck of the draw had paired Woods with Mark O'Meara in the third round. Although they are close friends, the pairing hadn't brought him much luck. Playing the seventh hole in 2001, one of Lytham's par 5s, Woods scored 7, two over par. Now, playing the fifth, Muirfield's first par 5, he scored another 7, even though for the first time that day he drove in the fairway. His second shot squirted into the right rough, he chopped out in 3, overshot the green in 4, chipped on in 5, and two putts later had his 7. Four over par for the day, Woods was seven strokes behind Els.

On and on it went. Through the first nine, Woods hit only two fairways and three greens, played the first eight holes in six over par, and went out in 42.

Starting back, he played the 10th through the 14th in five over par, a string that included a 5 on the 13th, a par 3 where he took two strokes from a greenside pot bunker.

By then the weather had eased, and Woods finally birdied a hole. After running in a putt from five feet for a 4 on the 17th, he broke into a wide grin, raised both arms in triumph, took off his cap, turned towards the gallery, and bowed. Through it all he had kept perspective.

When he walked between the giant grandstands bordering both sides of the 18th fairway, the remaining fans cheered as if he had won, even though his final putt for a birdie ended as so many had through these three difficult days—it hit the hole and spun out.

At 219 for 54 holes, he had sunk to a tie for 67th place, one stroke ahead of Mickelson, which was nothing

Tiger Woods was out in 42 after this putt at the ninth.

Taking two strokes from the greenside bunker, Woods had 5 on the par-3 13th hole.

A *Love-Hate*
Relationship with the Open

Colin Montgomerie's relationship with the Open Championship might be described as love-hate. He would love to win it but hates his record. In 12 previous Opens, Monty had achieved just one top 10 finish, at Turnberry in 1994. When he missed the cut in 1992 at Muirfield, it was the first of five times in seven years that he failed to qualify for the weekend. Rounds of 74 and 64 in this year's championship meant the Scot, now 39 years of age, was playing late on Saturday afternoon.

It was the worst possible time. The rain lashed down and the wind, from the north, gusted to over 20 miles an hour. Monty kept one trend going: He scored 84, a record-equalling 20 strokes worse than his previous round. Monty was not the only player to suffer. Lee Janzen also had 84, while there were 81s from David Toms, the USPGA champion, and even Tiger Woods, his worst round ever as a professional.

For a Scot, Montgomerie does not have a good reputation as a wind player. He is associated with Troon, where his father was secretary for many years, but he learnt his golf in Yorkshire, far from the sea.

An 81 in the final round scuppered his chances at the Scottish Open at Carnoustie in 1996. It was on an earlier day in that tournament that he was asked, "Was the wind a factor?" His hair was blown wildly, the press tent in which he was sitting was creaking violently. After he had got over the absurdity of the question, he confirmed that, yes, the wind had been a factor.

Montgomerie managed to save par on each of the first three holes but then turned into the teeth of the gale. He dropped a shot at the short fourth and another at the par-5 fifth, where he almost shanked a recovery from the rough across the fairway—clubs were slipping in the players' hands—and had to hit a driver from the fairway for his fourth shot.

He bogeyed the sixth and double-bogeyed the eighth to be out in 41, then came home in 43. There was another double bogey at the 10th and pars only at the 14th and 15th holes.

Unlike Woods, he did not speak after his round. His explanation was that reporters outside the recorder's hut at the time were talking to Woods. A 75 on Sunday left him in 82nd place out of 83 players.

Clearly, this time he had read the newspapers. "I didn't storm off," he said. "I'm really hurt."

—Andy Farrell

new. In truth, everyone behind him felt a great weight lift.

It didn't matter to Montgomerie, though, that Woods was accumulating such a high score. Midway through his round, with the strokes piling up, Monty's shoulders slumped, his head drooped, and his disappointment was obvious.

Montgomerie matched the greatest difference in scoring from one round to another on record for the Open for those who completed all four rounds, the 20-stroke difference between his second and third rounds.

While Woods and Montgomerie were playing themselves out of the championship, Els, Smyth, and Harrington took turns claiming the lead.

Harrington surged ahead first, birdieing the first hole and moving to seven under par, and after both Smyth and Els fumbled at the start, he held a clear two-stroke lead. Sadly for him, Harrington couldn't hold on. His game unravelled at the fourth. His tee shot caught the rough, his recovery ran over the green, his next shot ran far past the hole, and two putts later he had 5 and dropped into a tie with Els, who had just started. Harrington followed with four more bogeys, went out in 41, shot 76, and dropped to a tie for 10th.

Maruyama birdied the first as well and went seven under, but he took

Colin Montgomerie made par on the 15th, but finished with three bogeys.

Els Stays Calm in the Eye of the Storm

Quotes from a stormy Saturday at the 2002 Open:

- "To have broken 76 or 77 today would have been a hell of a score, the way the weather conditions were."
- "I've seen it be calm in the mornings, blow in the afternoons, but I've never seen it like this."
- "I was quite surprised on the front nine. We kept dropping shots and they wouldn't take us off the leaderboard ... So I knew at that stage, nobody was really having a lot of fun."

This was Ernie Els, after a day that had dawned grey and cool, and degenerated into a relentless downpour and a ripping wind before easing very late in the afternoon.

"The guys who were playing in the morning, if they knew what we had this afternoon," Els said, "I'm sure they would have played harder ... Some of those guys could have been leading right now."

There were 10 scores in the 80s, including 84 by Colin Montgomerie and an even more surprising 81 by Tiger Woods.

Muirfield yielded four 68s in the peaceful morning. Then the dark skies opened, the wind raged, and the scores soared. Going out, Els laboured to 40 strokes in the teeth of the storm. "At that stage, the only playable holes were the downwind holes, and most of them were on the back nine," he said.

Els bogeyed the second hole, three-putting from 50 feet. "It's tough for me to putt when it's really blowing a lot," the tall South African said. He parred the third, then suffered three straight bogeys.

At the 212-yard fourth, Els tried a two iron, which he usually hits 235 yards. He couldn't reach the green. At the par-5 fifth, he barely got to the fairway off the tee, and at the sixth, he was in rough off the tee, and short and still in the rough with his approach shot.

It was during this grind that Els realised what a tough time everyone was having. He and Shigeki Maruyama were bogeying left and right, but they never budged from the leaderboard.

The weather eased when he reached the second nine, and he jumped at his chance. He got four strokes back on birdies for a round of 40-32–72. Only 17 scores were better, and Els had a two-stroke lead over Soren Hansen, in second place.

The birdies had brought Els back, but it was a par that saved him. After the beating he took on the first nine, he needed something to hold himself together. He got it on the 10th green. He sent his first putt six feet past the hole, but made the return putt to salvage a par.

"I think I could have lost my composure," Els said, "if I didn't make that little putt."

—*Marino Parascenzo*

6 on the second, shot 75, but still tied for third.

The struggle through most of the day centred around Smyth and Els.

Smyth had come into the Open with no great expectations and no intention of continuing to battle young lions who consistently belted the ball 50 yards past him. He looked forward more towards joining the seniors tour in 2003, when he would turn 50. Yet for most of the day he played better than all those young big hitters.

Smyth had relied on solid driving and good putting through his 30-year career. In two rounds he had hit 20 of the 28 fairways on driving holes and 29 of the 36 greens, and while his putting could have been better, he had shot two solid rounds of 68 and 69. Now here he was, bundled against the cold in a heavy jacket and woolen cap, battling—and beating—men nearly half his age.

Paired with Carl Pettersson, who hadn't yet reached his 25th birthday, Smyth drove into a bunker on the first, three-putted, and opened with a 6, giving up two strokes to par. He also took a bogey at the eighth, but birdied the par-5 ninth, and played the first nine in 38. Five holes later, faced with a 15-footer to take the lead, Smyth rolled it in and dropped to four under, one stroke in front.

Els had gone out in 40 by then and fallen from six under at the start to only two under after nine. Starting back, he picked up a stroke on the 11th by holing a monster putt of 45 feet from across the green so perfectly gauged that, had his target been a painted circle, the ball would have stopped in the exact centre.

Els caught Smyth moments later with another well-judged putt from 20 feet on the 13th that died as it dropped, but he bunkered his drive and bogeyed the 14th. Smyth was ahead once more.

Some spectators stayed on a cruise ship in the Firth of Forth.

Soren Hansen's 73 moved him into second place and in Sunday's final group.

Round Three Hole Summary

HOLE	PAR	EAGLES	BIRDIES	PARS	BOGEYS	D. BOGEYS	HIGHER	RANK	AVERAGE
1	4	0	11	38	29	5	0	5	4.34
2	4	0	17	50	14	2	0	16	4.01
3	4	0	13	53	15	2	0	14	4.07
4	0	0	8	52	22	2	1	6	3.29
5	5	1	14	43	18	5	2	9	5.22
6	4	0	5	41	31	4	2	2	4.49
7	3	0	7	66	7	3	0	14	3.07
8	4	0	9	50	20	2	2	7	4.27
9	5	2	39	36	6	0	0	18	4.55
OUT	36	3	121	429	162	25	7		37.31
10	4	0	0	32	46	5	0	1	4.68
11	4	0	9	55	18	1	0	11	4.13
12	4	0	11	61	11	0	0	17	4.00
13	3	0	4	45	28	6	0	3	3.43
14	4	1	10	56	14	1	1	13	4.08
15	4	0	9	53	20	1	0	10	4.16
16	3	0	6	51	24	2	0	7	3.27
17	5	0	19	41	18	4	1	12	5.12
18	4	0	2	49	26	6	0	3	4.43
IN	35	1	70	443	205	26	2		37.30
TOTAL	71	4	191	872	367	51	9		74.61

Two bogeys at the end left Des Smyth in a tie for third place.

Smyth finally broke on the last two holes. His drive on the 17th dived into heavy rough, his recovery pulled up 180 yards or so short of the green, and his third squirted into the rough once again. The ball settled so close to the edge of a deep, greenside bunker, Smyth couldn't take a solid stance. Instead, he balanced himself on no more than the balls of his feet, and after a number of practice swings, pitched on. Because of his awkward stance, he had left himself a long putt for the par, but, nonetheless, it almost dropped. Instead, he bogeyed.

Three under now, tied with Els, Smyth moved to the home hole. After a two iron to the fairway, he pushed his three iron towards the right greenside bunker. Here he had a break. Instead of dropping into the sand, his ball settled on a grass-covered island, leaving him a decent lie. He pitched on nicely but missed a holeable putt from four feet, the kind he had to hole to stay in contention.

The USPGA champion, David Toms, shot 81 and was at the back of the field.

Back in 36, Smyth shot 74 and 211.

Now Els took charge. A par on the 15th, then a five iron to five feet on the 16th. The putt fell, and Els was four under now and back in front. On to the 17th. Two big shots to the green, then two putts from 35 feet for another birdie.

Five under par once more and two strokes clear of the field, Els drilled a drive down the 18th fairway, played a five iron to the front of the green, and got down in 2. After his laboured start he had turned his game around, come back in 32, and could go into the last round with a slight cushion.

The pin flags were finally tucked away.

Excerpts from the
Press

"Muirfield has been a joyful contrast to the huge expanses of Augusta and Bethpage State Park, the venues for the opening two majors of the year. It is a true risk and reward course."

—**Mark Reason**,
The Sunday Telegraph

"It was a day when one astonishing story superseded another."

—**Doug Proctor**, *The Sunday Post*

"It was fitting that the man who took greatest advantage of Woods's problems was Ernie Els, the South African who could probably have dominated any other era but that in which the American has reigned."

—**Alasdair Reid**, *The Sunday Times*

"The sight of spectators leaving the course in droves even before Woods had racked up a 7 at the fifth hole spoke volumes for the conditions experienced by the afternoon second-round leaders."

—**Alan Campbell**, *Sunday Herald*

"On a windswept, cold and rainy Scottish afternoon, the elements did to Woods what so many pressure situations could not. Woods fell apart. His game collapsed in shocking fashion, each errant shot leading to another."

—**Clifton Brown**,
The New York Times

'Big Easy' Wins The Hard Way

By Robert Sommers

When the Open Championship was last at Muirfield in 1992, Ernie Els was playing in the championship for the first time as a professional. This was the summer after John Daly had become prominent in August of 1991 by winning the USPGA Championship and launching drives that soared towards outer space and left orbit only after flights of 300 yards or more.

The following July, Daly showed up at Muirfield for his introduction to the Open and wowed the galleries once more with his uncommon length. Fans waited near a crosswalk 300 yards or more from Muirfield's 17th tee one day to see how far Daly's tee shot would carry. When they saw a ball run through the walkway and stop a few yards beyond, they assumed it had been Daly's drive. Instead, they watched as a tall, young

Ernie Els was in the Open's 16th playoff, the first with four players.

South African strode past. With that long, liquid swing, it was clear this young man—one whom they came to call "Big Easy"—could play this game.

This was Els, then 22 years of age, on his way to an opening round of 66. A few minutes later, Daly's drive stopped short of the crosswalk, and he shot 74. Els, who had first played in the 1989 Open as an amateur, shot 279 that week and tied for fifth. Daly shot 298 and placed last among those completing 72 holes.

Over the next 10 years, Els won two US Opens, an accomplishment in itself, but never the Open Championship. He had tied for second and third in the previous two Opens, but he had never won, and that wasn't good enough. Even Daly had pulled himself together long enough to win the 1995 Open. But not Ernie—not until he returned to Muirfield in 2002.

Under strange circumstances even for this old championship, Els shot 278, six under par, and won a four-man playoff, beating Frenchman Thomas Levet and two Australians, Steve Elkington and Stuart Appleby.

The Open had been around since 1860 and had seen many a playoff, but never one between four men. The last previous playoff, strangely enough, had involved Jean Van de Velde, another Frenchman. In the entire

Excerpts from the
Press

"Ernie Els stood in the fading sunlight as the bagpipes played, feeling relief as much as joy. Holding the trophy and holding his emotions, Els insisted this time, without Tiger Woods but not without the most unusual playoff in tournament history, might be his last time to win the Open."

—Art Spander, *Oakland Tribune*

"Gary Evans was all too aware of the history of the Open ... and for a time yesterday the European tour journeyman, who has never won a tournament as a professional, was on the brink of joining that distinguished company. It was, of course, the most unnerving experience of his life."

—Tim Glover, *The Independent*

"All his life, Ernie Els had thought about emulating his idol, fellow South African Gary Player, by winning the Open. But as Els walked dejectedly off the 16th green at Muirfield, the only thought on his mind was what others would say if he lost."

—Joe Juliano, *Philadelphia Inquirer*

"The Frenchman was wonderful, waving his arms to get the crowd noise up, cupping his hand to his ear to say he couldn't hear them. He was loving it."

—Bill Leckie, *The Sun*

"The playoff was more a test of nerve than a test of ability."

—David McCarthy, *Daily Record*

Playing his second shot to No 17, Padraig Harrington birdied here then bogeyed 18.

history of the Open, Arnaud Massy had been the only French champion, and he had won in 1907, beating J.H. Taylor by two. After he lost a playoff to Harry Vardon in 1911, Massy muttered, "I cannot play this game."

Els could, and he never should have been taken to a playoff. One stroke ahead of Elkington, Appleby, and Levet as he stepped onto the 16th tee, he moved to the 17th one stroke behind them. Mis-playing two chip shots after missing the green, Els double-bogeyed.

He rallied himself on the 17th, played two fine shots to the green, and two-putted for the birdie that pulled him even. Then he won the playoff with a marvellous recovery from a greenside bunker at the 18th and beat Levet by one stroke in sudden death. Both Appleby and Elkington had been eliminated over the stipulated playoff round of four holes.

Els closed with 70 after earlier rounds of 70, 68, and 72, but Appleby won his place with a blistering final round of 65, and both Elkington and Levet shot 66, for this had been a day of unusually low scoring. Harrington played stirring golf and shot 67, but he had bogeyed the 18th and fallen one stroke short at 279.

The weather had eased from Saturday's miserable conditions, which had prompted Duffy Waldorf to claim, "About the sixth hole I wasn't sure my life would go on."

The morning overcast cleared, the sun shone bright, sweaters came off, and scores dropped. At the end, 36 players had shot in the 60s, and

SUNDAY WEATHER
Temperature: low 12°C, high 17°C.
Light northerly breeze.

The 18th hole of the Open Championship always provides a dramatic setting.

another 13 had broken par 71. Only 25 of the 83 starters failed either to break or match par. High for the day, Welshman David Park shot 80, eating up an impressive percentage of his strokes on the 13th. Park's vagrant tee shot plunged into the same pot bunker where Tiger Woods had taken two to escape Saturday. Park would have settled for Tiger's double bogey, because once in, he took seven useless flails before breaking his shackles with the eighth, the embodiment of the fabled angry man and his wedge. After two putts and some complex mathematics, he put down 11 on the scorecard, the only double-digit hole of the championship.

Meantime, Colin Montgomerie and David Toms, both of whom shot in the 80s Saturday, teed off at 7.45 and sprinted round Muirfield in two hours and 40 minutes. Both men shot 75. Montgomerie's 297 beat only Toms, whose 298 placed him last.

While Montgomerie appeared focused on getting out of town, Woods played for pride and for the outside chance he might frighten the leaders and by some miracle snatch the championship. He sped round in 65 and finished with 284, level par, not nearly good

Greg Norman finished four strokes behind and said the difference was his putting.

Peter O'Malley shot 65 and climbed into a share of eighth place, two strokes behind.

Missed putts and a 69 left Sergio Garcia joint eighth.

enough to catch up, but it confirmed his desire.

Playing directly behind him, Pierre Fulke matched his 284 by shooting 65 as well, and a few pairs later, Australian Peter O'Malley shot his own 65. Starting only an hour before Els and Soren Hansen, who teed off at 2.30, Appleby shot his 65 later in the day, scorching the second nine with a closing 30, polished off by birdies on the 15th, 17th, and 18th. He came very close to shooting 28, but missed birdieing the 13th from three feet and missed still another short putt on the 16th.

Woods had come to win, and he would do his best so long as he had holes to play. Playing every shot for all he could squeeze from it, he had given all he had to give and the gallery saw it. When he took off his cap and shook hands with Jeff Maggert, his pairing mate, they cheered a championship attitude.

About an hour later the fans had the feeling they might be cheering a championship effort, because, like Woods, Fulke, and O'Malley before him, Gary Evans began tearing into Muirfield, and if not for a wild drive on the home hole, he might have made it a five-man playoff.

A 33-year-old Englishman, Evans had never been a power in European golf. He had played 274 tournaments without winning any, but by the time he had passed the 16th, there was ample evidence his day might have come.

Paired with Scott Verplank, Evans began the round tied for 23rd place after opening with 72, 68, and 74. While Verplank fell back to tie for 37th place with his level-par 71, Evans began climbing, and, indeed, played a level of golf not often seen. Beginning at the second, he played 10 holes in eight under par, scoring seven 3s, one 2, one 4, and one 5.

First-class ball-striking consistently set up birdie openings, and Evans used them. He holed from 12 feet on the second, from less than a foot on the third, from four feet on the sixth, from 15 feet on the par-3 seventh, and from five feet on the eighth. Reaching the fifth green with his second shot, he two-putted for still another birdie.

Out in 31, Evans kept his streak going by holing a huge putt of about 80 feet on the 10th, and ended his remarkable run with a pitch to 12 feet and his eighth birdie on the 11th. He had gone from one over par to six under, leading the Open Championship.

Evans still had seven hard holes to play, and hard as he tried, he couldn't pick up another stroke. His round reached its climax on the 17th, a hole

After having lost a golf ball at the 17th, Gary Evans (above) holed an improbable 40-foot putt for par.

Retief Goosen, who shot 67, thought he would need 64 or 65—and was right.

he felt he could reach with his second shot for a certain birdie and perhaps an eagle 3. His drive split the fairway, and then he lashed into a fairway wood and yanked the ball left towards Muirfield's impossible rough.

Every blade of grass that has ever grown off those fairways is still there. It has never been cut; it just bends over, eventually dies, and new grass takes its place. Evans's ball carried into that maze and burrowed out of sight.

More than two dozen spectators rushed in and searched, but it was lost.

Evans walked back, played a good shot to the green, and against all logic, holed a putt from at least 40 feet to save par. A sizeable gallery had rushed

Round of the Day

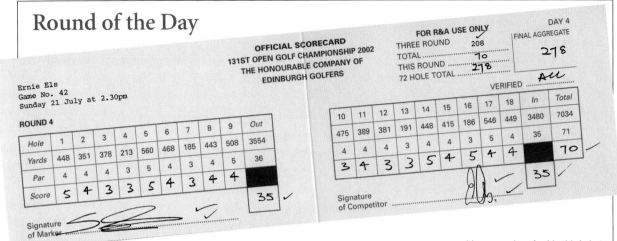

OFFICIAL SCORECARD
131ST OPEN GOLF CHAMPIONSHIP 2002
THE HONOURABLE COMPANY OF
EDINBURGH GOLFERS

FOR R&A USE ONLY
THREE ROUND 208
TOTAL 70
THIS ROUND 278
72 HOLE TOTAL ....

DAY 4
FINAL AGGREGATE
278

VERIFIED .... All

Ernie Els
Game No. 42
Sunday 21 July at 2.30pm

ROUND 4

Hole	1	2	3	4	5	6	7	8	9	Out
Yards	448	351	378	213	560	468	185	443	508	3554
Par	4	4	4	3	5	4	3	4	4	36
Score	5	4	3	3	5	4	3	4	4	35 ✓

Signature of Marker

10	11	12	13	14	15	16	17	18	In	Total
475	389	381	191	448	415	186	546	449	3480	7034
4	4	4	3	4	4	3	5	4	35	71
3	4	3	3	5	4	5	4	4		70 ✓

Signature of Competitor

35 ✓

Despite a bogey on the first hole and a double bogey on the 16th, Ernie Els won the Open Championship with a round of 70 for a total of 278, six under par, which earned him a berth in the playoff.

Els hit a wedge to 30 feet for his first birdie on the par-4 third hole. He reached the green of the par-5 ninth with a two iron on his second shot and took two putts from 35 feet. A seven iron to 12 feet resulted in a birdie at the par-4 10th hole, and Els hit a wedge to the green and holed an 18-foot putt for birdie at the par-4 12th.

He took bogey at the par-4 14th after hitting into a bunker off the tee, reaching the green with a seven iron for his third shot and two-putting from 18 feet. Disaster struck at the par-3 16th, as Els's seven-iron shot went left off the tee and he missed his mark with a sand wedge through the green, then took three more strokes for 5. But Els came back to birdie the par-5 17th from 20 feet, then won on the fifth playoff hole.

to him by then, and when the putt fell, the cheering must have been heard in North Berwick, to the east. He was still six under with only the home hole left.

He was spent. He hit shots into the right rough, into the left grandstand, and holed a desperate 10-footer to save a bogey 5. Five under now, he had shot 65 and had played 18 holes with only 23 putts.

Stepping off the green, Evans took off his cap and wiped his forehead, emotionally exhausted. He had put a score of 279 on the board; it was up to the others to match it. His had been a gallant effort, but, again, it wasn't good enough. Two others did indeed match it, and four others beat it.

With Muirfield yielding to a surge of exceptional shotmaking, the field grew tightly bunched. At one stage, nine men had closed within one stroke of one another, but one by one they lost strokes, until at the end only four remained.

Hansen began two strokes behind Els and shot 70, making up no ground at all. Harrington reached six under par by birdieing the 17th, but bogeyed the 18th and fell to five under, one too many. Thomas Bjorn stumbled to start with a double bogey 6, and his 69 was two strokes too high. Scott Hoch shot 66, but needed two strokes fewer. Peter O'Malley had started too far back for his 65 to catch up. Retief Goosen needed something better than his 67. Sergio Garcia's closing 69 left him two strokes behind. Perhaps his age had caught

It's a Fact

This was the 12th appearance by Ernie Els in the Open Championship. When Nick Price won in 1994 at Turnberry, it was his first victory in 16 appearances, a record for the years since 1963 when the entire field has not had to play qualifying rounds. Mark O'Meara won in 1998 at Royal Birkdale in his 14th appearance.

Excerpts from the
Press

"There is not a single member of the golf-writing corps who, in their heart of hearts, would not sooner work with a Montgomerie than any of those emotion-free souls who talk about taking 'one shot at a time.'"

—Lewine Mair, *The Daily Telegraph*

"Scot Andrew Coltart eased his way home to another substantial pay day, then took time out to salute the real winners—the fans."

—Niall Aitcheson, *Daily Mail*

"Padraig Harrington effectively dropped the old claret jug in a bunker on the 18th hole yesterday. The Irishman was not to know it at the time, but standing on the tee of the final hole a par down the last would have been enough to secure him a place in the playoff."

—Jamie Wilson, *The Guardian*

"The most nervous person on the course was their Belgian sports psychologist Jos Vanstiphout, who works with both players (Els and Levet)."

—Tony Stenson, *Daily Mirror*

"Ernie Els finally fulfilled his date with destiny to win the Open—but wife Liezl couldn't bear to watch. Mrs. Els buried her face in an official's shoulder as her hubby sank the four-foot putt that clinched the most coveted prize in golf."

—Bill Thornton, *Daily Star*

After his 66, Scott Hoch called Muirfield his favourite Open Championship venue.

up, but Des Smyth shot 73, one of the day's higher rounds, and Justin Leonard shot 70, Scott McCarron 71, and Justin Rose 72, far too many. There would be neither a Swedish, nor an American, nor an Irish, nor a Spanish, nor a Danish, nor an English champion.

Until the very end it seemed equally unlikely we would see another French champion, for after a promising first nine of 33, Levet had stalled. He had birdied the second and third, Muirfield's shortest par-4 holes, and added another at the ninth, where he reached the green with a four-iron second shot. Four under now, he came back playing a series of frustrating par holes until the 17th. After a useful drive, Levet ripped a two iron to the back of the green, and from a ridiculous range, about 45 feet, holed for an eagle 3. At six under, Levet had caught Appleby, who had just finished. Now Arnaud Massy's reincarnation seemed possible.

For a time at least, a Japanese golfer looked destined to become the Open champion. Beginning at two under par, three strokes behind Els, Shigeki Maruyama, the happiest man at Muirfield, surrendered the almost obligatory bogey on the first, but he followed up by birdieing four of the next five holes. When he added another at the ninth, he had gone out in 32, four under par and six under for 63 holes. He had gone in front, for Els, playing four groups behind, had made no headway and was still five under.

Good Result for an Emotional Favourite

Each time Stuart Appleby returns to the Open Championship, the 31-year-old Australian must have to deal with emotions few other players experience. A day after the 1998 Open at Royal Birkdale, where Appleby missed the cut, he and his wife, Renay, were due to travel by Eurostar from Waterloo train station in London to Paris for a short romantic break. In a freak accident, a taxi reversed into Renay and she died a short time later.

In New South Wales, the Renay Appleby Memorial Trophy each year recognises the state's best female junior golfer.

Despite the personal trauma, Appleby's career continues to progress, although it has not always been easy. Until the Western Open two weeks before the Open, his run of appearing in every major since 1997 was in danger. But he finished fifth there to gain one of the exemptions on offer at the tournament from The Royal and Ancient Golf Club. "The Western Open was my little gold nugget," said Appleby, who was raised on an outback dairy farm. "Otherwise it was qualifying. I wanted to keep my run going."

At Muirfield, he took advantage of avoiding the worst of the weather on Saturday to close with rounds of 70 and 65, in which he came home in 30 with birdies at the last two holes, to set the clubhouse target of six under par that eventually got him into the four-man playoff.

"I was feeling nervous from the very first hole," Appleby said of the final round. "I was nervous all day but I guess it was good nerves, more of a stimulus than anything else. I made the putts I hadn't made all week. I was a few laps behind and I had to put the foot to the floor. I didn't have time to look behind me."

In the playoff he took 4 at the 16th but recovered the shot with a birdie at the 17th. But his chance disappeared with a bogey at the last when he found a greenside bunker and only just got the ball out with his recovery. "So near, so far, I guess," Appleby said. "You know, it was good fun. It was a good experience this week. I got into a playoff and did not play near my best at all."

At the prize-giving Els said a few words about each of the runners-up. Of Appleby he said simply, "He's got the talent." The implication was that one day the young Aussie could be standing where Els was at that moment.

—*Andy Farrell*

Although missing this putt on the 11th, Stuart Appleby posted 65 with a blistering 30 on the last nine.

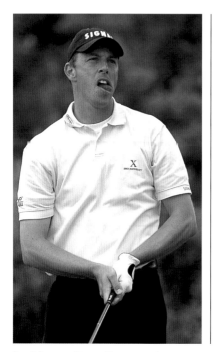

Danish stars Soren Hansen (left) and Thomas Bjorn were among six tied at 280. Hansen was pleased with his result. But Bjorn looked back to his double bogey on the first hole.

Wearing his customary beaming grin between holes —he's all business playing his shots— Maruyama suddenly began losing ground. He three-putted the 10th, played the 11th nicely for a routine par, then drove into the right rough of the 12th, missed the green to the left, barely escaping a bunker, played a loose chip, and bogeyed once more. Four under now, he three-putted the 13th; he was finished.

Maruyama picked up birdies on the 16th and 17th, but his 68 and 279 total, five under par, fell one stroke short. Still, as he walked off the 18th green, his beaming smile outshone the sun.

Later, when a friend asked about those few loose holes, Maruyama confessed he couldn't remember anything from the 11th through the 14th holes.

Maruyama had been paired with Elkington, who had been lucky to make the field. He had come over to qualify at Dunbar, about 20 miles farther along the East Lothian coast. Apparently safe playing his approach to the last hole, Elkington knocked his ball out of bounds when his iron hit an embedded stone. He would have faced a playoff, three men for two places, but an exempt player, Paul Azinger, had withdrawn, allowing for another place, and Elkington was in.

Allergies and injuries had bothered Elkington since the 1995 season, when he had won the USPGA Championship in Los Angeles and later in the year lost to Els in the final match of the World Match Play at Wentworth. Elkington had barely made the cut in the Open, playing the first 36 holes in 144. Putting had never been his strength, otherwise he might have won the Open in 72 holes, because he played such steady, inspiring golf on the way to his 66. Nevertheless, he had missed a number of holeable putts, especially two on the

Fourth Round Leaders

HOLE	1	2	3	4	5	6	7	8	9	10	11	12	13	14	15	16	17	18	
PAR	4	4	4	3	5	4	3	4	5	4	4	4	3	4	4	3	5	4	TOTAL
Ernie Els	[5]	4	(3)	3	5	4	3	4	(4)	(3)	4	(3)	3	[5]	4	[5]	(4)	4	70-278
Stuart Appleby	4	4	4	[4]	(4)	4	3	4	(4)	(3)	4	(3)	3	4	(3)	3	(4)	(3)	65-278
Thomas Levet	4	(3)	(3)	3	5	4	3	4	(4)	4	4	4	3	4	4	3	(3)	4	66-278
Steve Elkington	4	4	4	(2)	5	4	3	(3)	(4)	4	(3)	4	3	4	4	3	(4)	4	66-278
Gary Evans	[5]	(3)	(3)	3	(4)	(3)	(2)	(3)	5	(3)	(3)	4	3	4	4	3	5	[5]	65-279
Padraig Harrington	4	4	4	3	(4)	4	(2)	(3)	5	4	4	4	3	4	(3)	3	(4)	[5]	67-279
Shigeki Maruyama	[5]	(3)	(3)	3	(4)	(3)	3	4	(4)	[5]	4	[5]	[4]	4	4	(2)	(4)	4	68-279
Peter O'Malley	4	(3)	4	3	5	4	3	4	(3)	(3)	(3)	(3)	3	4	[5]	(2)	5	4	65-280
Scott Hoch	4	(3)	4	3	5	4	(2)	(3)	(4)	4	4	4	3	(3)	4	3	(4)	[5]	66-280
Retief Goosen	4	4	(3)	(2)	(4)	[5]	3	4	(4)	4	4	4	3	4	[5]	(2)	(4)	4	67-280
Thomas Bjorn	[6]	(3)	4	[4]	5	4	3	4	(4)	4	(3)	4	3	4	(3)	3	(4)	4	69-280
Sergio Garcia	4	4	(3)	3	(4)	[5]	3	4	5	4	4	4	3	4	(3)	3	5	4	69-280
Soren Hansen	4	4	4	(2)	5	4	3	4	(4)	4	4	4	3	4	[5]	3	(4)	[5]	70-280

Shigeki Maruyama called his week at the Open "a great experience."

Low Scores

Low First Nine

Gary Evans	31

Low Second Nine

Stuart Appleby	30

Low Round

Peter O'Malley	65
Tiger Woods	65
Stuart Appleby	65
Pierre Fulke	65
Gary Evans	65

Players Below Par	49
Players At Par	9
Players Above Par	25

Championship Totals	
Players Below Par	153
Players At Par	51
Players Above Par	271

Elkington Plays Like His Old Self

Ask Jackie Burke about Steve Elkington and the crusty old professional from Elkington's home course, Champions Golf Club in Houston, Texas, will stare you in the eyes and say his protégé is a hypochondriac. Burke, the 1956 Masters champion, is of course joking. But, if anyone wanted to follow the punchline of the old joke and have as his tombstone epitaph: "I told you I was sick," it would be Elkington.

The sweet-swinging Australian, who has made his home in Texas since attending the University of Houston, has a medical history that would fill a full season of a television hospital show. Allergic to grass, Elkington has had a history of sinus problems. And in the last two years he has had a sore back, a sore wrist and hip surgery. But he played the Open at Muirfield as if he were trying to prove the axiom: Life begins at 40.

Elkington started the week as a qualifier, playing his way in at Dunbar, and ended it with a share of second place after playing the weekend rounds in only 134 strokes—66 in the final round.

"I played basically a perfect round," Elkington said on Sunday. "I never mis-hit a shot. I hit every fairway and every green. I played a great round of golf."

For Elkington, who had six top 10 finishes in major championships before 1996—including a victory at the 1995 USPGA—had finished in the top 10 only once since in majors, that being in the 1998 USPGA. Moreover, since finishing tied for sixth in the 1995 Open Championship, he had missed the cut four times, withdrawn once, and tied for 60th the only time he finished 72 holes.

"It's really fun for me," Elkington said about his bounce back. "It's the reason why I love golf so much, to be over here, be in Scotland, see all the other guys trying to qualify. I made it and almost won the Open. It's kind of what it's all about. It's why they call it the Open. Everybody has a chance to do it."

Playing in the first two-ball of the four-man playoff, Elkington was the first to fall, failing to get up-and-down from the back fringe on the fourth and final hole of the playoff format. Still, he was able to look ahead rather than dwell on the missed opportunity.

"I would have liked to go back in that playoff," he said. "I was hitting it so straight. I would have liked another crack at it (the four-iron approach shot in the playoff that went through the green). "No one is playing better than I am. I don't care who it is. No one is swinging better than I am. I really made a big breakthrough."

—Ron Sirak

closing holes. He missed the first of those from no more than six feet behind the hole on the 15th, and two holes later his putt for an eagle 3 on the 17th lipped out. With a holeable putt to go to seven under on the 18th, he missed once again.

Still, Elkington had played 18 holes over a severely testing course without a bogey and without a 5 on his scorecard. Six under par, he had caught Appleby and Levet at 278; now they would wait for Els, who had birdied the ninth and gone six under par, beginning what looked to be a runaway sprint to the championship.

Els stepped onto the 10th tee just one of a bunch within a stroke of one another, but Ernie quickly opened a gap. His seven-iron approach ran about six inches off the back of the 10th green, but he holed the 12-foot putt. He was now seven under par.

His drive in the rough, he still hit the 11th green and parred, then birdied the 12th and slipped eight under.

Els seemed safe now. Three strokes ahead of the field, he could play the remaining six holes in level par and assure a clear victory, something he hadn't tasted on one of the big occasions since 1997, when he had won his second US Open.

Nothing came easy. Appleby had birdied the 18th to go six under and cut Ernie's lead to two strokes, and Els looked at risk when he bunkered his tee shot to the little 13th, but from an awkward stance, he pitched out inside a foot, one of the more remarkable shots of the championship. One hole later he slipped on the 14th, driving into a fairway bunker and taking a bogey. Seven under now, Els still had one stroke in hand. A steady par on the 15th, and then he stepped onto the tee of the par-3 16th hole.

Throughout the day, Els had tended to pull his irons, and here his tee shot settled left of the green at the base of a downgrade. Facing what looked to be a simple pitch-and-run up a slope to the flagstick, Els bladed the shot. The ball squirted up the hill, ran past the hole, slowed its speed, then gently glided down an

Steve Elkington missed several holeable putts including one from just four feet (above left) to win on the 72nd hole. He bogeyed there in the playoff.

Round Four Hole Summary

HOLE	PAR	EAGLES	BIRDIES	PARS	BOGEYS	D. BOGEYS	HIGHER	RANK	AVERAGE
1	4	0	4	52	23	3	1	1	4.34
2	4	0	20	63	0	0	0	15	3.76
3	4	0	19	59	5	0	0	13	3.83
4	3	0	13	54	16	0	0	8	3.04
5	5	1	30	47	5	0	0	16	4.68
6	4	0	11	56	13	2	1	5	4.11
7	3	0	11	60	10	2	0	8	3.04
8	4	0	16	60	7	0	0	11	3.89
9	5	4	43	34	1	1	0	18	4.42
OUT	**36**	**5**	**167**	**485**	**80**	**8**	**2**		**35.10**
10	4	0	7	50	23	3	0	3	4.27
11	4	0	19	60	4	0	0	14	3.82
12	4	0	19	58	6	0	0	12	3.84
13	3	0	15	56	9	2	1	6	3.07
14	4	0	4	55	22	2	0	3	4.27
15	4	0	14	50	18	1	0	6	4.07
16	3	0	12	59	11	1	0	10	3.01
17	5	1	42	35	5	0	0	17	4.53
18	4	0	4	55	20	4	0	2	4.29
IN	**35**	**1**	**136**	**478**	**118**	**13**	**1**		**35.17**
TOTAL	**71**	**6**	**303**	**963**	**198**	**21**	**3**		**70.26**

Victory seemed to be slipping away from Els at the 18th.

incline perhaps eight yards or so off the green. From there he took three more strokes and strode to the 17th tee one stroke behind.

Now Els faced the prospect that once again he had thrown away a great chance to win something of importance. He would certainly have to birdie one of the last two holes, and the 17th would be easier than the 18th. He ripped into a drive, had only a four iron left, flew it to the green, left his first putt dangerously short, but holed the second. Six under, he had caught up. On to the final hole.

Avoiding the two fairway bunkers in the drive zone, Els played an iron, then a five iron to the back of the green within holing distance. Once again he left the putt short. When the ball stopped rolling, Els hung his head, wondering if he had thrown away the Open Championship. But he made it.

After Els checked and signed his scorecard, he would join Levet, Elkington, and Appleby for the four-hole playoff over the first, 16th, 17th, and 18th holes.

Elkington and Levet teed off first, followed by Els and Appleby in the second pairing. The playoff became just as tense as the finish. Elkington bogeyed the first and 18th and stepped aside, and Appleby bogeyed the

No French Victory, and No Regrets

Annually at Wimbledon the home crowd gets terribly worked up in the hope of a British player winning the men's singles championship for the first time since Fred Perry in 1936. In France it is probably not *chic* to worry that no golfer from their country has won the Open Championship since Arnaud Massy at Hoylake in 1907. There are signs, however, that golf is taking more of a root in the country.

On the eve of this year's championship, the man from *Le Figaro* was pleasantly surprised with the number of words he was being asked to produce. The increased interest may be driven by *Le Tigre*, but it can do no harm that for the second time in four Opens a Frenchman came close to lifting the silver claret jug.

Thomas Levet found himself in a four-way playoff thanks to a final round of 66 in which the 33-year-old Parisian did not drop a shot and was the only man to eagle the 17th. With a 45-foot curling putt at the 16th hole, Levet took the lead in the stroke-play playoff, but after driving into the rough and then hitting into a bunker, he bogeyed the last to tie with Ernie Els. When he bogeyed the 18th again, this time driving into a bunker, but only just missing his putt for par, the drama was over.

Levet had won a four-way playoff at the British Masters at Woburn in 2001.

Just before that playoff had started, he found a ball-marker with the picture of a shamrock, which he still carried.

His luck finally ran out, but not before enjoying the greatest day of his golfing life. He smiled his way down the 18th fairway and waved to the gallery. "I am very happy with what I did today," Levet said. "It was a great day. I don't regret anything. I wouldn't change my approach. I had a chance at the last, but I didn't play the 18th well enough."

Levet had started the day hoping to get into contention and, by finishing in the top 15, earn an exemption into the Open for next year. He did not get the exemption to the age of 65 for winning, but he would have to change his schedule to play at the USPGA Championship at Hazeltine a few weeks later.

Jean Van de Velde, who needed 6 at the last at Carnoustie and took 7, ended a comic-tragic figure in 1999. Here Levet proved the most gracious of runners-up. "I lost to a great player," he said. "He's a big man, very talented." When Els holed the winning putt, his celebrations were helped on their way by "Levetation" as the Frenchman lifted the victor into the air.

—Andy Farrell

Championship Hole Summary

HOLE	PAR	EAGLES	BIRDIES	PARS	BOGEYS	D. BOGEYS	HIGHER	RANK	AVERAGE
1	4	0	34	260	154	26	1	1	4.37
2	4	0	115	315	41	4	0	16	3.86
3	4	0	87	335	51	2	0	14	0.00
4	3	0	42	316	105	10	2	6	3.19
5	5	11	135	251	61	14	3	15	4.88
6	4	0	48	260	139	23	5	3	4.33
7	3	0	53	352	59	10	1	11	3.06
8	4	0	52	311	103	7	2	9	4.15
9	5	14	227	198	29	5	2	18	4.56
OUT	**36**	**25**	**793**	**2598**	**742**	**101**	**16**		**36.33**
10	4	0	25	278	152	18	2	2	4.36
11	4	0	99	310	60	6	0	13	3.94
12	4	0	64	349	57	5	0	12	4.01
13	3	0	53	312	94	14	2	7	3.17
14	4	1	39	300	121	12	2	5	4.23
15	4	0	63	307	94	9	2	10	4.12
16	3	0	37	330	100	8	0	8	3.17
17	5	6	182	226	50	7	4	17	4.75
18	4	0	37	302	114	21	1	4	4.26
IN	**35**	**7**	**599**	**2714**	**842**	**100**	**13**		**36.00**
TOTAL	**71**	**32**	**1392**	**5312**	**1584**	**201**	**29**		**72.32**

Thomas Levet struck first with a birdie on the 16th hole in the playoff.

Elkington was left with an eight-foot putt and took 5.

Appleby barely got his third shot out of the bunker.

16th and 18th and joined him. Both had birdied the 17th, so they finished with 17 strokes, one over par. Els, meanwhile, parred every hole, and Levet birdied the 16th, bogeyed the 18th, and at level-par 16, joined Els for sudden death on the 18th.

All Ernie's years of struggle came down to one dangerous 449-yard hole. If he failed, he might never regain the confidence he would need to win another championship.

Here Levet made a mistake. Going with a driver, he ran his ball into a fairway bunker, and Els looked as if he had won. But once again Els pulled an iron shot that dived into the left greenside bunker.

With only his left foot in the sand and his right bent at an awkward angle on the bank outside, Els played a wonderful shot. The ball popped out and ran within about four feet of the hole. Levet had a putt of seven feet for a matching par, but he missed.

When Ernie's putt fell, he smiled for the first time that day, secure in knowing that after five lean years, he had finally won another of the game's great challenges.

Summing it all up later, Ernie said, "I've been after this for 10 years. If I hadn't got it this year, I don't think I'd have made it. I've had a fabulous time, but it's been very hard."

Playoff

HOLE	1	16	17	18	Total	Extra Hole 18
PAR	4	3	5	4		4
Ernie Els	4	3	5	4	16	4
Thomas Levet	4	②	5	⑤	16	⑤
Stuart Appleby	4	④	④	⑤	17	
Steve Elkington	⑤	3	④	⑤	17	

Playing a great bunker shot, Els had a short putt to win.

The Biggest Test of All

By John Hopkins

What was Ernie Els thinking of? What on earth had he just done? Had he momentarily taken leave of his senses? He, of all people, the man who seems so hard to ruffle, whose temperament seems as balanced as his swing is smooth, appeared to have thrown away victory in the Open Championship.

It was teatime on Sunday, a calm day of almost unbroken sunshine. With that long, steady walk of his, Els appeared to be striding to victory in the Open. He had dropped one stroke on the 14th, which was serious but not disastrous. Then he dropped two more on the 16th, chipping from one side of the green to the other. Suddenly, the two-stroke lead he had held with five holes of his last round remaining had gone. Suddenly, he was one stroke behind. What would happen now?

Before the Marines award their famous green berets to the young men who have survived months of demanding training, they test these men to the full, both their bodies and their brains. The final tests last for 24 hours during which no sleep is allowed. The thinking behind this is that it is when a person is most stretched physically and mentally that he reveals his true nature.

In a not dissimilar way Els was being tested to the full now. He had never before faced a situation like this. He was the most experienced player left in contention, the best, the highest-ranked in the world. For once in a major championship, Tiger Woods was not in contention. Yet Els seemed to have thrown away one of the precious few chances players get to win. How would he react to his mistakes on the 14th and 16th holes?

It took only a couple of minutes, the time needed for Els to walk from the 16th green back to the 17th tee for him to form a battle plan in his mind. What would one give to have been able to read his mind in those few minutes? I suspect his language would have been blue as he railed at himself for his mistakes. I also suspect however that once the railing was over, he used every mental technique he could find to transform himself into the frame of mind necessary to play the next two holes in one under par to join Steve Elkington, Stuart Appleby, and Thomas Levet in the playoff.

This is precisely what he did. His swing on the 17th tee appeared more languid than ever—no sign of pressure there—and powered his tee shot into a good position on the fairway, and from there another, perhaps even better, shot found the green. Two putts there gave him the birdie that drew him back to level with the other three leaders at six under par.

Els later revealed how he composed himself before his drive on the 17th. He questioned himself, wondering whether he wanted to be known as a man who had thrown away a major championship. Then he asked himself if he could live with that? The answers to both questions were no.

So he made sure he got his par at the last playoff hole, and then made sure he hit his drive down the middle of the fairway on the first hole of sudden death against Levet. But once again, Els let loose his grip on the claret jug and once again he had to summon all his skill and mental fortitude to regain it. From a drive into the middle of the fairway, he hit his second shot into a greenside bunker and had to play his third stroke with his left leg in the sand and his right leg on the grass outside the bunker.

Would Els have made so many mistakes earlier in his career, in the days before he was beaten so often by Woods and before he grew tired of hearing the name of the world's No 1? Perhaps not. Yet perhaps the fact that he made these mistakes and then recovered from them was a signal that Els is now a stronger man than he was. He had demonstrated before the last round that his technical expertise was beyond compare at this Open, coping with the wind and rain better than Woods had. Perhaps this victory would reinforce Els's belief in himself?

If that does indeed become the case, then Els has to thank Jos Vanstiphout, the Belgian mind coach, with whom he had worked for a year. Vanstiphout is a small, friendly man who smokes ceaselessly, a figure one sees around the fringes. His influence among players on the European Tour is considerable—and growing.

"Ernie had not won for 18 months when I started with him," Vanstiphout said. "Like 90 percent of the players, he had a bad case of Tiger Woods-itis. We had to work on his self-belief and his self-esteem. He has always had a good swing, a knife through butter. And now he has finally got the mental side back again so that he can not just compete in every major championship but against Woods every time."

There was evidence of a change in Els's attitude in the heady moments after the Open. "I pulled myself together and made some good shots," Els said. "I guess I've got a little bit of fight in me when it counts."

That fight earned him a third major championship to go with the US Opens of 1994 and 1997. People had been saying that Els was too good not to be winning major championships. Perhaps the man himself realised that at Muirfield, and perhaps now he will start to win more.

The Open Championship

Results

Year	Champion	Score	Margin	Runners-up	Venue
1860	Willie Park Snr	174	2	Tom Morris Snr	Prestwick
1861	Tom Morris Snr	163	4	Willie Park Snr	Prestwick
1862	Tom Morris Snr	163	13	Willie Park Snr	Prestwick
1863	Willie Park Snr	168	2	Tom Morris Snr	Prestwick
1864	Tom Morris Snr	167	2	Andrew Strath	Prestwick
1865	Andrew Strath	162	2	Willie Park Snr	Prestwick
1866	Willie Park Snr	169	2	David Park	Prestwick
1867	Tom Morris Snr	170	2	Willie Park Snr	Prestwick
1868	Tom Morris Jnr	154	3	Tom Morris Snr	Prestwick
1869	Tom Morris Jnr	157	11	Bob Kirk	Prestwick
1870	Tom Morris Jnr	149	12	Bob Kirk, David Strath	Prestwick
1871	*No Competition*				
1872	Tom Morris Jnr	166	3	David Strath	Prestwick
1873	Tom Kidd	179	1	Jamie Anderson	St Andrews
1874	Mungo Park	159	2	Tom Morris Jnr	Musselburgh
1875	Willie Park Snr	166	2	Bob Martin	Prestwick
1876	Bob Martin	176	—	David Strath	St Andrews
	(Martin was awarded the title when Strath refused to play-off)				
1877	Jamie Anderson	160	2	Bob Pringle	Musselburgh
1878	Jamie Anderson	157	2	Bob Kirk	Prestwick
1879	Jamie Anderson	169	3	James Allan, Andrew Kirkaldy	St Andrews
1880	Bob Ferguson	162	5	Peter Paxton	Musselburgh
1881	Bob Ferguson	170	3	Jamie Anderson	Prestwick
1882	Bob Ferguson	171	3	Willie Fernie	St Andrews
1883	Willie Fernie	158	Playoff	Bob Ferguson	Musselburgh
1884	Jack Simpson	160	4	Douglas Rolland, Willie Fernie	Prestwick
1885	Bob Martin	171	1	Archie Simpson	St Andrews
1886	David Brown	157	2	Willie Campbell	Musselburgh
1887	Willie Park Jnr	161	1	Bob Martin	Prestwick
1888	Jack Burns	171	1	David Anderson Jnr, Ben Sayers	St Andrews
1889	Willie Park Jnr	155	Playoff	Andrew Kirkaldy	Musselburgh
1890	*John Ball Jnr	164	3	Willie Fernie, Archie Simpson	Prestwick
1891	Hugh Kirkaldy	166	2	Willie Fernie, Andrew Kirkaldy	St Andrews
(From 1892 the competition was extended to 72 holes)					
1892	*Harold Hilton	305	3	*John Ball Jnr, Hugh Kirkaldy, Sandy Herd	Muirfield

Sandy Lyle (1985)

Justin Leonard (1997)

Year	Champion	Score	Margin	Runners-up	Venue
1893	Willie Auchterlonie	322	2	*John Laidlay	Prestwick
1894	J.H. Taylor	326	5	Douglas Rolland	Sandwich
1895	J.H. Taylor	322	4	Sandy Herd	St Andrews
1896	Harry Vardon	316	Playoff	J.H. Taylor	Muirfield
1897	*Harold Hilton	314	1	James Braid	Hoylake
1898	Harry Vardon	307	1	Willie Park Jnr	Prestwick
1899	Harry Vardon	310	5	Jack White	Sandwich
1900	J.H. Taylor	309	8	Harry Vardon	St Andrews
1901	James Braid	309	3	Harry Vardon	Muirfield
1902	Sandy Herd	307	1	Harry Vardon, James Braid	Hoylake
1903	Harry Vardon	300	6	Tom Vardon	Prestwick
1904	Jack White	296	1	James Braid, J.H. Taylor	Sandwich
1905	James Braid	318	5	J.H. Taylor, Rowland Jones	St Andrews
1906	James Braid	300	4	J.H. Taylor	Muirfield
1907	Arnaud Massy	312	2	J.H. Taylor	Hoylake
1908	James Braid	291	8	Tom Ball	Prestwick
1909	J.H. Taylor	295	6	James Braid, Tom Ball	Deal
1910	James Braid	299	4	Sandy Herd	St Andrews
1911	Harry Vardon	303	Playoff	Arnaud Massy	Sandwich
1912	Ted Ray	295	4	Harry Vardon	Muirfield
1913	J.H. Taylor	304	8	Ted Ray	Hoylake
1914	Harry Vardon	306	3	J.H. Taylor	Prestwick

1915-1919 No Championship

Year	Champion	Score	Margin	Runners-up	Venue
1920	George Duncan	303	2	Sandy Herd	Deal
1921	Jock Hutchison	296	Playoff	*Roger Wethered	St Andrews
1922	Walter Hagen	300	1	George Duncan, Jim Barnes	Sandwich
1923	Arthur Havers	295	1	Walter Hagen	Troon
1924	Walter Hagen	301	1	Ernest Whitcombe	Hoylake
1925	Jim Barnes	300	1	Archie Compston, Ted Ray	Prestwick
1926	*Robert T. Jones Jnr	291	2	Al Watrous	Royal Lytham
1927	*Robert T. Jones Jnr	285	6	Aubrey Boomer, Fred Robson	St Andrews
1928	Walter Hagen	292	2	Gene Sarazen	Sandwich
1929	Walter Hagen	292	6	John Farrell	Muirfield
1930	*Robert T. Jones Jnr	291	2	Leo Diegel, Macdonald Smith	Hoylake

Year	Champion	Score	Margin	Runners-up	Venue
1931	Tommy Armour	296	1	Jose Jurado	Carnoustie
1932	Gene Sarazen	283	5	Macdonald Smith	Prince's
1933	Densmore Shute	292	Playoff	Craig Wood	St Andrews
1934	Henry Cotton	283	5	Sid Brews	Sandwich
1935	Alf Perry	283	4	Alf Padgham	Muirfield
1936	Alf Padgham	287	1	Jimmy Adams	Hoylake
1937	Henry Cotton	290	2	Reg Whitcombe	Carnoustie
1938	Reg Whitcombe	295	2	Jimmy Adams	Sandwich
1939	Richard Burton	290	2	Johnny Bulla	St Andrews

1940-1945 No Championship

Year	Champion	Score	Margin	Runners-up	Venue
1946	Sam Snead	290	4	Bobby Locke, Johnny Bulla	St Andrews
1947	Fred Daly	293	1	Reg Horne, *Frank Stranahan	Hoylake
1948	Henry Cotton	284	5	Fred Daly	Muirfield
1949	Bobby Locke	283	Playoff	Harry Bradshaw	Sandwich
1950	Bobby Locke	279	2	Roberto de Vicenzo	Troon
1951	Max Faulkner	285	2	Tony Cerda	Royal Portrush
1952	Bobby Locke	287	1	Peter Thomson	Royal Lytham
1953	Ben Hogan	282	4	*Frank Stranahan, Dai Rees, Peter Thomson, Tony Cerda	Carnoustie
1954	Peter Thomson	283	1	Sid Scott, Dai Rees, Bobby Locke	Royal Birkdale
1955	Peter Thomson	281	2	Johnny Fallon	St Andrews
1956	Peter Thomson	286	3	Flory van Donck	Hoylake
1957	Bobby Locke	279	3	Peter Thomson	St Andrews
1958	Peter Thomson	278	Playoff	David Thomas	Royal Lytham
1959	Gary Player	284	2	Flory van Donck, Fred Bullock	Muirfield
1960	Kel Nagle	278	1	Arnold Palmer	St Andrews
1961	Arnold Palmer	284	1	Dai Rees	Royal Birkdale
1962	Arnold Palmer	276	6	Kel Nagle	Troon
1963	Bob Charles	277	Playoff	Phil Rodgers	Royal Lytham
1964	Tony Lema	279	5	Jack Nicklaus	St Andrews
1965	Peter Thomson	285	2	Christy O'Connor, Brian Huggett	Royal Birkdale
1966	Jack Nicklaus	282	1	David Thomas, Doug Sanders	Muirfield
1967	Roberto de Vicenzo	278	2	Jack Nicklaus	Hoylake
1968	Gary Player	289	2	Jack Nicklaus, Bob Charles	Carnoustie
1969	Tony Jacklin	280	2	Bob Charles	Royal Lytham
1970	Jack Nicklaus	283	Playoff	Doug Sanders	St Andrews

Mark O'Meara (1998)

David Duval (2001)

Paul Lawrie (1999)

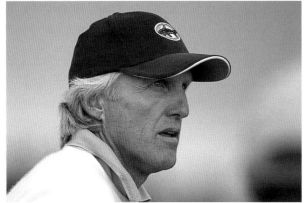

Greg Norman (1986, 1993)

John Daly (1995)

Year	Champion	Score	Margin	Runners-up	Venue
1971	Lee Trevino	278	1	Lu Liang Huan	Royal Birkdale
1972	Lee Trevino	278	1	Jack Nicklaus	Muirfield
1973	Tom Weiskopf	276	3	Neil Coles, Johnny Miller	Troon
1974	Gary Player	282	4	Peter Oosterhuis	Royal Lytham
1975	Tom Watson	279	Playoff	Jack Newton	Carnoustie
1976	Johnny Miller	279	6	Jack Nicklaus, Severiano Ballesteros	Royal Birkdale
1977	Tom Watson	268	1	Jack Nicklaus	Turnberry
1978	Jack Nicklaus	281	2	Simon Owen, Ben Crenshaw, Raymond Floyd, Tom Kite	St Andrews
1979	Severiano Ballesteros	283	3	Jack Nicklaus, Ben Crenshaw	Royal Lytham
1980	Tom Watson	271	4	Lee Trevino	Muirfield
1981	Bill Rogers	276	4	Bernhard Langer	Sandwich
1982	Tom Watson	284	1	Peter Oosterhuis, Nick Price	Royal Troon
1983	Tom Watson	275	1	Hale Irwin, Andy Bean	Royal Birkdale
1984	Severiano Ballesteros	276	2	Bernhard Langer, Tom Watson	St Andrews
1985	Sandy Lyle	282	1	Payne Stewart	Sandwich
1986	Greg Norman	280	5	Gordon J. Brand	Turnberry
1987	Nick Faldo	279	1	Rodger Davis, Paul Azinger	Muirfield
1988	Severiano Ballesteros	273	2	Nick Price	Royal Lytham
1989	Mark Calcavecchia	275	Playoff	Greg Norman, Wayne Grady	Royal Troon
1990	Nick Faldo	270	5	Mark McNulty, Payne Stewart	St Andrews
1991	Ian Baker-Finch	272	2	Mike Harwood	Royal Birkdale
1992	Nick Faldo	272	1	John Cook	Muirfield
1993	Greg Norman	267	2	Nick Faldo	Sandwich
1994	Nick Price	268	1	Jesper Parnevik	Turnberry
1995	John Daly	282	Playoff	Costantino Rocca	St Andrews
1996	Tom Lehman	271	2	Mark McCumber, Ernie Els	Royal Lytham
1997	Justin Leonard	272	3	Jesper Parnevik, Darren Clarke	Royal Troon
1998	Mark O'Meara	280	Playoff	Brian Watts	Royal Birkdale
1999	Paul Lawrie	290	Playoff	Justin Leonard, Jean Van de Velde	Carnoustie
2000	Tiger Woods	269	8	Ernie Els, Thomas Bjorn	St Andrews
2001	David Duval	274	3	Niclas Fasth	Royal Lytham
2002	Ernie Els	278	Playoff	Thomas Levet, Stuart Appleby, Steve Elkington	Muirfield

*Denotes amateurs

The Open Championship

Records

MOST VICTORIES
6, Harry Vardon, 1896-98-99-1903-11-14
5, James Braid, 1901-05-06-08-10; J.H. Taylor, 1894-95-1900-09-13; Peter Thomson, 1954-55-56-58-65; Tom Watson, 1975-77-80-82-83

MOST TIMES RUNNER-UP OR JOINT RUNNER-UP
7, Jack Nicklaus, 1964-67-68-72-76-77-79
6, J.H. Taylor, 1896-1904-05-06-07-14

OLDEST WINNER
Old Tom Morris, 46 years 99 days, 1867
Harry Vardon, 44 years 41 days, 1914
Roberto de Vicenzo, 44 years 93 days, 1967

YOUNGEST WINNER
Young Tom Morris, 17 years 5 months 8 days, 1868
Willie Auchterlonie, 21 years 24 days, 1893
Severiano Ballesteros, 22 years 3 months 12 days, 1979

YOUNGEST AND OLDEST COMPETITOR
Young Tom Morris, 14 years 4 months 4 days, 1865
Gene Sarazen, 74 years 5 months 8 days, 1976

BIGGEST MARGIN OF VICTORY
13 strokes, Old Tom Morris, 1862
12 strokes, Young Tom Morris, 1870
11 strokes, Young Tom Morris, 1869
8 strokes, J.H. Taylor, 1900 and 1913; James Braid, 1908; Tiger Woods, 2000

LOWEST WINNING AGGREGATES
267 (66, 68, 69, 64), Greg Norman, Royal St George's, 1993
268 (68, 70, 65, 65), Tom Watson, Turnberry, 1977; (69, 66, 67, 66), Nick Price, Turnberry, 1994
269 (67, 66, 67, 69), Tiger Woods, St Andrews, 2000

Tiger Woods (2000)

LOWEST AGGREGATE IN RELATION TO PAR
269 (19 under par), Tiger Woods, St Andrews, 2000
270 (18 under par), Nick Faldo, St Andrews, 1990

LOWEST AGGREGATES BY RUNNER-UP
269 (68, 70, 65, 66), Jack Nicklaus, Turnberry, 1977; (69, 63, 70, 67), Nick Faldo, Royal St George's, 1993; (68, 66, 68, 67), Jesper Parnevik, Turnberry, 1994

LOWEST AGGREGATES BY AN AMATEUR
281 (68, 72, 70, 71), Iain Pyman, Royal St George's, 1993; (75, 66, 70, 70), Tiger Woods, Royal Lytham, 1996

LOWEST INDIVIDUAL ROUND
63, Mark Hayes, second round, Turnberry, 1977; Isao Aoki, third round, Muirfield, 1980; Greg Norman, second round, Turnberry, 1986; Paul Broadhurst, third round, St Andrews, 1990; Jodie Mudd, fourth round, Royal Birkdale, 1991; Nick Faldo, second round, and Payne Stewart, fourth round, Royal St George's, 1993

LOWEST INDIVIDUAL ROUND BY AN AMATEUR
66, Frank Stranahan, fourth round, Troon, 1950; Tiger Woods, second round, Royal Lytham, 1996; Justin Rose, second round, Royal Birkdale, 1998

LOWEST FIRST ROUND
64, Craig Stadler, Royal Birkdale, 1983; Christy O'Connor Jnr., Royal St George's, 1985; Rodger Davis, Muirfield, 1987; Raymond Floyd and Steve Pate, Muirfield, 1992

LOWEST SECOND ROUND
63, Mark Hayes, Turnberry, 1977; Greg Norman, Turnberry, 1986; Nick Faldo, Royal St George's, 1993

Nick Price (1994)

LOWEST THIRD ROUND
63, Isao Aoki, Muirfield, 1980; Paul Broadhurst, St Andrews, 1990

LOWEST FOURTH ROUND
63, Jodie Mudd, Royal Birkdale, 1991; Payne Stewart, Royal St George's, 1993

LOWEST FIRST 36 HOLES
130 (66, 64), Nick Faldo, Muirfield, 1992

LOWEST SECOND 36 HOLES
130 (65, 65), Tom Watson, Turnberry, 1977; (64, 66), Ian Baker-Finch, Royal Birkdale, 1991; (66, 64), Anders Forsbrand, Turnberry, 1994

LOWEST MIDDLE 36 HOLES
130 (66, 64), Fuzzy Zoeller, Turnberry, 1994

LOWEST FIRST 54 HOLES
198 (67, 67, 64), Tom Lehman, Royal Lytham, 1996
199 (67, 65, 67), Nick Faldo, St Andrews, 1990; (66, 64, 69), Nick Faldo, Muirfield, 1992

LOWEST FINAL 54 HOLES
199 (66, 67, 66), Nick Price, Turnberry, 1994

LOWEST 9 HOLES
28, Denis Durnian, first 9, Royal Birkdale, 1983
29, Peter Thomson and Tom Haliburton, first 9, Royal Lytham, 1958; Tony Jacklin, first 9, St Andrews, 1970; Bill Longmuir, first 9, Royal Lytham, 1979; David J. Russell, first 9, Royal Lytham, 1988; Ian Baker-Finch and Paul Broadhurst, first 9, St Andrews, 1990; Ian Baker-Finch, first 9, Royal Birkdale, 1991; Paul McGinley, first 9, Royal Lytham, 1996; Ernie Els, first 9, Muirfield, 2002

SUCCESSIVE VICTORIES
4, Young Tom Morris, 1868-72 (no championship in 1871).
3, Jamie Anderson, 1877-79; Bob Ferguson, 1880-82, Peter Thomson, 1954-56
2, Old Tom Morris, 1861-62; J.H. Taylor, 1894-95; Harry Vardon, 1898-99; James Braid, 1905-06; Bobby Jones, 1926-27; Walter Hagen, 1928-29; Bobby Locke, 1949-50; Arnold Palmer, 1961-62; Lee Trevino, 1971-72; Tom Watson, 1982-83

VICTORIES BY AMATEURS
3, Bobby Jones, 1926-27-30
2, Harold Hilton, 1892-97
1, John Ball, 1890
Roger Wethered lost a playoff in 1921

CHAMPIONS IN FIRST APPEARANCE
Willie Park, Prestwick, 1860; Tom Kidd, St Andrews, 1873; Mungo Park, Musselburgh, 1874; Harold Hilton, Muirfield, 1892; Jock Hutchison, St Andrews, 1921; Densmore Shute, St Andrews, 1933; Ben Hogan, Carnoustie, 1953; Tony Lema, St Andrews, 1964; Tom Watson, Carnoustie, 1975

BIGGEST SPAN BETWEEN FIRST AND LAST VICTORIES
19 years, J.H. Taylor, 1894-1913
18 years, Harry Vardon, 1896-1914
15 years, Gary Player, 1959-74
14 years, Henry Cotton, 1934-48

BIGGEST SPAN BETWEEN VICTORIES
11 years, Henry Cotton, 1937-48

CHAMPIONS IN THREE DECADES
Harry Vardon, 1896, 1903, 1911
J.H. Taylor, 1894, 1900, 1913
Gary Player, 1959, 1968, 1974

Nick Faldo (1987, 1990, 1992)

HIGHEST NUMBER OF TOP-FIVE FINISHES
16, J.H. Taylor, Jack Nicklaus
15, Harry Vardon, James Braid

HIGHEST NUMBER OF ROUNDS UNDER PAR
61, Jack Nicklaus
47, Nick Faldo
39, Tom Watson

HIGHEST NUMBER OF AGGREGATES UNDER PAR
14, Jack Nicklaus
13, Nick Faldo

MOST CONSECUTIVE ROUNDS UNDER 70
7, Ernie Els, 1993-94

OUTRIGHT LEADER AFTER EVERY ROUND
Ted Ray, 1912; Bobby Jones, 1927; Gene Sarazen, 1932; Henry Cotton, 1934; Tom Weiskopf, 1973

LEADER AFTER EVERY ROUND INCLUDING TIES
Harry Vardon, 1899 and 1903; J.H. Taylor, 1900; Lee Trevino, 1971; Gary Player, 1974

RECORD LEADS (SINCE 1892)
After 18 holes:
4 strokes, James Braid, 1908; Bobby Jones, 1927; Henry Cotton, 1934; Christy O'Connor Jnr., 1985
After 36 holes:
9 strokes, Henry Cotton, 1934
After 54 holes:
10 strokes, Henry Cotton, 1934
7 strokes, Tony Lema, 1964

BIGGEST LEADS BY NON-CHAMPIONS
After 54 holes:
5 strokes, Macdonald Smith, 1925; Jean Van de Velde, 1999

Mark Calcavecchia (1989)

CHAMPIONS WITH EACH ROUND LOWER THAN PREVIOUS ONE
Jack White, 1904, Sandwich, (80, 75, 72, 69)
James Braid, 1906, Muirfield, (77, 76, 74, 73)
Henry Cotton, 1937, Carnoustie, (74, 73, 72, 71)
Ben Hogan, 1953, Carnoustie, (73, 71, 70, 68)
Gary Player, 1959, Muirfield, (75, 71, 70, 68)

CHAMPION WITH FOUR ROUNDS THE SAME
Densmore Shute, 1933, St Andrews, (73, 73, 73, 73) (excluding the playoff)

BIGGEST VARIATION BETWEEN ROUNDS OF A CHAMPION
14 strokes, Henry Cotton, 1934, second round 65, fourth round 79
11 strokes, Jack White, 1904, first round 80, fourth round 69; Greg Norman, 1986, first round 74, second round 63, third round 74

BIGGEST VARIATION BETWEEN TWO ROUNDS (Competitors Who Completed Four Rounds)
20 strokes, R.G. French, 1938, second round 71, third round 91; Colin Montgomerie, 2002, second round 64, third round 84
19 strokes, R.H. Pemberton, 1938, second round 72, third round 91
18 strokes, A. Tingey Jnr., 1923, first round 94, second round 76
17 strokes, Jack Nicklaus, 1981, first round 83, second round 66; Ian Baker-Finch, 1986, first round 86, second round 69

BEST COMEBACK BY CHAMPIONS
After 18 holes:
Harry Vardon, 1896, 11 strokes behind the leader
After 36 holes:
George Duncan, 1920, 13 strokes behind the leader
After 54 holes:
Paul Lawrie, 1999, 10 strokes behind the leader

CHAMPIONS WITH FOUR ROUNDS UNDER 70
Greg Norman, 1993, Royal St George's, (66, 68, 69, 64); Nick Price, 1994, Turnberry, (69, 66, 67, 66); Tiger Woods, 2000, St Andrews, (67, 66, 67, 69)
Of non-champions:
Ernie Els, 1993, Royal St George's, (68, 69, 69, 68); Jesper Parnevik, 1994, Turnberry, (68, 66, 68, 67)

BEST FINISHING ROUND BY A CHAMPION
64, Greg Norman, Royal St George's, 1993
65, Tom Watson, Turnberry, 1977; Severiano Ballesteros, Royal Lytham, 1988; Justin Leonard, Royal Troon, 1997

WORST ROUND BY A CHAMPION SINCE 1939
78, Fred Daly, third round, Hoylake, 1947
76, Paul Lawrie, third round, Carnoustie, 1999

WORST FINISHING ROUND BY A CHAMPION SINCE 1939
75, Sam Snead, St Andrews, 1946

BEST OPENING ROUND BY A CHAMPION
66, Peter Thomson, Royal Lytham, 1958; Nick Faldo, Muirfield, 1992; Greg Norman, Royal St George's, 1993

BIGGEST RECOVERY IN 18 HOLES BY A CHAMPION
George Duncan, Deal, 1920, was 13 strokes behind the leader, Abe Mitchell, after 36 holes and level after 54

MOST APPEARANCES
46, Gary Player
37, Jack Nicklaus

MOST APPEARANCES ON FINAL DAY (SINCE 1892)
32, Jack Nicklaus
31, Alex Herd
30, J.H. Taylor
27, Harry Vardon, James Braid
26, Peter Thomson, Gary Player
23, Dai Rees
22, Henry Cotton

MOST APPEARANCES BEFORE FIRST VICTORY
16, Nick Price, 1994
14, Mark O'Meara, 1998

MOST APPEARANCES WITHOUT A VICTORY
29, Dai Rees
28, Sam Torrance
27, Neil Coles

CHAMPIONSHIP WITH HIGHEST NUMBER OF ROUNDS UNDER 70
148, Turnberry, 1994

CHAMPIONSHIP SINCE 1946 WITH THE FEWEST ROUNDS UNDER 70
St Andrews, 1946; Hoylake, 1947; Portrush, 1951; Hoylake, 1956; Carnoustie, 1968. All had only two rounds under 70.

LONGEST COURSE
Carnoustie, 1999, 7361 yards

COURSES MOST OFTEN USED
St Andrews, 26; Prestwick, 24; Muirfield, 15; Sandwich, 12; Hoylake and Royal Lytham, 10; Royal Birkdale, 8; Royal Troon, 7; Musselburgh and Carnoustie, 6; Turnberry, 3; Deal, 2; Royal Portrush and Prince's, 1

Tom Lehman (1996)

Tom Watson (1975, 1977, 1980, 1982, 1983)

Prize Money

Year	Total	First Prize	Year	Total	First Prize	Year	Total	First Prize
1860	nil	nil	1991	900,000	90,000	1997	1,586,300	250,000
1863	10	nil	1992	950,000	95,000	1998	1,800,000	300,000
1864	15	6	1993	1,000,000	100,000	1999	2,000,000	350,000
1876	27	10	1994	1,100,000	110,000	2000	2,750,000	500,000
1889	22	8	1995	1,250,000	125,000	2001	3,300,000	600,000
1891	30.50	10	1996	1,400,000	200,000	2002	3,800,000	700,000
1892	100	35						
1893	100	30						
1910	135	50						
1920	225	75						
1927	275	75						
1930	400	100						
1931	500	100						
1946	1,000	150						
1949	1,500	300						
1953	2,500	500						
1954	3,500	750						
1955	3,750	1,000						
1958	4,850	1,000						
1959	5,000	1,000						
1960	7,000	1,250						
1961	8,500	1,400						
1963	8,500	1,500						
1965	10,000	1,750						
1966	15,000	2,100						
1968	20,000	3,000						
1969	30,334	4,250						
1970	40,000	5,250						
1971	45,000	5,500						
1972	50,000	5,500						
1975	75,000	7,500						
1977	100,000	10,000						
1978	125,000	12,500						
1979	155,000	15,000						
1980	200,000	25,000						
1982	250,000	32,000						
1983	310,000	40,000						
1984	445,000	50,000						
1985	530,000	65,000						
1986	634,000	70,000						
1987	650,000	75,000						
1988	700,000	80,000						
1989	750,000	80,000						
1990	825,000	85,000						

Attendance

Year	Attendance	Year	Attendance	Year	Attendance
1962	37,098	1976	92,021	1990	208,680
1963	24,585	1977	87,615	1991	189,435
1964	35,954	1978	125,271	1992	146,427
1965	32,927	1979	134,501	1993	141,000
1966	40,182	1980	131,610	1994	128,000
1967	29,880	1981	111,987	1995	180,000
1968	51,819	1982	133,299	1996	170,000
1969	46,001	1983	142,892	1997	176,000
1970	81,593	1984	193,126	1998	195,100
1971	70,076	1985	141,619	1999	157,000
1972	84,746	1986	134,261	2000	230,000
1973	78,810	1987	139,189	2001	178,000
1974	92,796	1988	191,334	2002	161,500
1975	85,258	1989	160,639		

The 131st Open Championship

Complete Scores

HOLE		1	2	3	4	5	6	7	8	9	10	11	12	13	14	15	16	17	18	
PAR		4	4	4	3	5	4	3	4	5	4	4	4	3	4	4	3	5	4	TOTAL
Ernie Els	Round 1	4	4	4	3	4	6	4	4	4	4	4	4	3	3	4	3	4	4	70
South Africa	Round 2	3	3	3	3	4	3	3	3	4	4	5	4	4	4	4	3	5	4	66
£700,000	Round 3	4	5	4	4	6	5	3	4	5	4	3	4	2	5	4	2	4	4	72
	Round 4	5	4	3	3	5	4	3	4	4	3	4	3	3	5	4	5	4	4	70 -278
	Playoff	4															3	5	4	16
	Extra Hole																4			
Thomas Levet	Round 1	4	4	4	3	5	5	3	4	5	5	4	4	2	5	4	3	4	4	72
France	Round 2	3	3	4	3	5	3	3	4	5	4	4	4	3	3	4	3	4	4	66
£286,667	Round 3	5	4	4	4	5	5	3	4	4	5	4	4	4	3	4	3	5	4	74
	Round 4	4	3	3	3	5	4	3	4	4	4	4	4	3	4	4	3	3	4	66 -278
	Playoff	4															2	5	5	16
	Extra Hole																	5		
Stuart Appleby	Round 1	4	4	4	3	5	4	3	4	5	5	4	4	3	4	5	3	4	5	73
Australia	Round 2	4	4	4	4	5	4	3	4	5	4	4	4	2	3	4	3	5	4	70
£286,667	Round 3	4	4	4	3	5	4	3	4	4	4	4	5	3	4	4	3	5	3	70
	Round 4	4	4	4	4	4	4	3	4	4	3	4	3	3	4	3	3	4	3	65 -278
	Playoff	4															4	4	5	17
Steve Elkington	Round 1	4	4	4	3	6	4	2	4	5	4	4	4	3	5	4	3	5	3	71
Australia	Round 2	5	3	4	3	5	3	3	5	5	5	4	4	4	4	4	3	5	4	73
£286,667	Round 3	4	3	3	4	4	4	3	4	5	4	5	4	3	4	3	3	4	4	68
	Round 4	4	4	4	2	5	4	3	3	4	4	3	4	3	4	4	3	4	4	66 -278
	Playoff	5															3	4	5	17
Gary Evans	Round 1	6	4	4	4	5	4	3	3	4	5	3	4	4	3	4	3	5	4	72
England	Round 2	4	4	4	2	5	4	3	4	5	4	3	3	3	5	3	3	4	5	68
£140,000	Round 3	5	4	4	3	6	3	3	4	4	5	5	3	3	4	3	4	6	5	74
	Round 4	5	3	3	3	4	3	2	3	5	3	3	4	3	4	4	3	5	5	65 -279
Padraig Harrington	Round 1	4	4	4	3	4	4	3	4	4	5	5	3	2	4	4	4	4	4	69
Ireland	Round 2	4	3	3	2	5	4	3	5	4	5	3	4	3	4	4	3	4	4	67
£140,000	Round 3	3	4	4	5	6	5	4	5	5	5	4	4	4	3	3	3	5	4	76
	Round 4	4	4	4	3	4	4	2	3	5	4	4	4	3	4	3	3	4	5	67 -279
Shigeki Maruyama	Round 1	4	3	4	3	4	4	3	3	4	4	4	4	3	5	4	3	5	4	68
Japan	Round 2	5	3	4	3	5	4	3	4	4	3	4	4	3	4	4	3	4	4	68
£140,000	Round 3	3	6	5	3	7	5	2	4	5	5	3	4	3	4	4	3	5	4	75
	Round 4	5	3	3	3	4	3	3	4	4	5	4	5	4	4	4	2	4	4	68 -279

*Denotes amateurs

HOLE		1	2	3	4	5	6	7	8	9	10	11	12	13	14	15	16	17	18	
PAR		4	4	4	3	5	4	3	4	5	4	4	4	3	4	4	3	5	4	TOTAL
Peter O'Malley	Round 1	5	3	4	3	4	8	3	4	4	4	4	4	3	4	3	3	5	4	72
Australia	Round 2	5	4	4	2	5	4	2	4	5	4	4	3	3	4	4	3	5	3	68
£77,500	Round 3	4	4	4	3	5	5	5	5	4	5	5	3	3	4	4	3	5	4	75
	Round 4	4	3	4	3	5	4	3	4	3	3	3	3	3	4	5	2	5	4	65 -280
Scott Hoch	Round 1	4	4	4	4	7	5	4	4	4	4	3	4	3	4	4	4	4	4	74
USA	Round 2	4	4	4	3	3	4	3	4	4	4	3	4	4	4	4	3	4	4	69
£77,500	Round 3	4	3	4	3	5	5	3	4	4	4	4	5	3	4	4	3	5	4	71
	Round 4	4	3	4	3	5	4	2	3	4	4	4	4	3	3	4	3	4	5	66 -280
Retief Goosen	Round 1	4	3	4	3	5	5	3	5	4	4	4	4	3	5	4	3	4	4	71
South Africa	Round 2	4	4	4	3	5	5	2	4	3	4	3	4	3	4	4	3	5	4	68
£77,500	Round 3	4	5	4	4	5	5	3	5	4	4	4	5	4	3	4	3	4	4	74
	Round 4	4	4	3	2	4	5	3	4	4	4	4	4	3	4	5	2	4	4	67 -280
Thomas Bjorn	Round 1	3	3	3	3	5	5	3	3	5	3	5	3	3	4	4	3	6	4	68
Denmark	Round 2	4	4	4	3	4	3	2	4	5	5	5	4	3	4	3	3	5	5	70
£77,500	Round 3	3	5	4	5	4	5	3	4	5	4	5	3	4	4	4	3	4	4	73
	Round 4	6	3	4	4	5	4	3	4	4	4	3	4	3	4	3	3	4	4	69 -280
Sergio Garcia	Round 1	5	4	3	3	6	4	5	4	5	4	3	3	3	4	4	3	4	4	71
Spain	Round 2	4	4	4	3	4	4	3	5	5	4	4	4	3	4	3	3	4	4	69
£77,500	Round 3	3	4	4	3	5	4	4	4	5	4	4	4	4	4	4	3	4	4	71
	Round 4	4	4	3	3	4	5	3	4	5	4	4	4	3	4	3	3	5	4	69 -280
Soren Hansen	Round 1	4	3	4	4	4	4	3	4	4	4	4	4	2	4	4	3	4	5	68
Denmark	Round 2	4	4	4	3	4	4	3	4	5	4	4	4	3	4	4	3	4	4	69
£77,500	Round 3	4	5	4	3	5	5	4	4	4	4	4	4	3	4	5	3	4	4	73
	Round 4	4	4	4	2	5	4	3	4	4	4	4	4	3	4	5	3	4	5	70 -280
Davis Love III	Round 1	4	4	4	4	5	4	3	3	5	4	4	4	3	4	5	3	4	4	71
USA	Round 2	5	3	4	3	5	5	4	4	4	5	4	4	2	4	4	3	4	5	72
£49,750	Round 3	5	3	4	3	5	4	3	4	5	5	3	4	3	4	4	3	5	4	71
	Round 4	4	3	4	3	4	4	3	3	5	4	4	4	2	4	4	3	5	4	67 -281
Nick Price	Round 1	4	3	4	3	6	5	3	3	5	4	3	3	3	4	4	3	4	4	68
Zimbabwe	Round 2	3	3	4	3	4	4	3	5	5	5	3	4	4	4	4	3	5	4	70
£49,750	Round 3	4	4	5	3	6	5	3	3	3	5	4	4	4	4	4	4	5	5	75
	Round 4	5	3	5	2	4	5	3	4	4	4	3	4	3	4	3	3	5	4	68 -281
Peter Lonard	Round 1	5	4	4	3	5	3	3	5	4	4	3	4	2	5	4	4	5	5	72
Australia	Round 2	5	3	4	3	4	4	3	5	7	4	3	4	3	4	6	3	4	3	72
£49,750	Round 3	4	3	3	2	3	5	3	3	6	5	4	4	3	4	4	3	5	4	68
	Round 4	4	4	3	2	5	4	3	5	3	4	4	5	3	5	4	3	4	4	69 -281
Justin Leonard	Round 1	4	4	4	3	4	5	3	4	4	4	4	4	3	5	3	4	5	4	71
USA	Round 2	4	5	4	3	5	3	2	5	6	4	3	4	3	6	5	2	5	3	72
£49,750	Round 3	4	4	4	3	5	5	3	4	4	4	4	3	3	3	4	3	4	4	68
	Round 4	5	4	4	3	5	3	3	4	4	4	3	4	3	4	5	3	5	4	70 -281
Bob Estes	Round 1	4	4	4	4	4	4	3	4	4	4	4	4	3	5	4	4	4	4	71
USA	Round 2	4	4	4	2	4	5	3	4	5	3	4	4	3	4	5	3	4	5	70
£41,000	Round 3	4	4	4	2	6	4	2	4	5	5	5	4	3	4	4	3	5	5	73
	Round 4	4	4	4	3	5	4	3	4	4	4	3	4	3	4	4	3	4	4	68 -282
Greg Norman	Round 1	4	4	5	3	4	4	2	4	4	5	5	4	4	4	4	4	4	3	71
Australia	Round 2	4	5	5	3	5	4	3	4	5	4	4	4	4	3	4	2	5	4	72
£41,000	Round 3	5	4	4	3	5	4	3	4	4	5	4	4	3	4	3	4	4	4	71
	Round 4	4	4	4	3	5	3	2	4	4	4	4	4	3	4	5	3	4	4	68 -282

HOLE		1	2	3	4	5	6	7	8	9	10	11	12	13	14	15	16	17	18	
PAR		4	4	4	3	5	4	3	4	5	4	4	4	3	4	4	3	5	4	TOTAL
Duffy Waldorf	Round 1	4	4	4	3	5	4	3	4	4	4	4	3	3	3	4	3	5	3	67
USA	Round 2	4	4	5	3	5	4	4	4	3	5	4	3	3	4	3	3	4	4	69
£41,000	Round 3	5	5	5	4	7	6	3	5	5	5	3	3	3	3	3	2	5	5	77
	Round 4	4	4	3	3	5	4	3	4	5	4	4	4	2	5	4	3	4	4	69 -282
Scott McCarron	Round 1	4	4	4	3	5	4	3	5	4	4	4	4	3	4	4	3	5	4	71
USA	Round 2	4	4	4	3	5	3	2	4	5	4	5	3	3	4	3	3	5	4	68
£41,000	Round 3	4	4	5	3	5	4	3	4	4	5	4	4	3	4	4	3	5	4	72
	Round 4	4	4	4	3	3	4	3	5	5	4	5	4	4	4	4	3	4	4	71 -282
Chris Riley	Round 1	3	3	4	4	5	5	3	4	4	4	4	4	2	4	6	3	4	4	70
USA	Round 2	6	4	4	2	4	4	4	4	5	4	3	4	3	4	5	3	4	4	71
£32,000	Round 3	4	4	4	3	6	4	3	5	4	4	4	4	3	4	5	4	6	5	76
	Round 4	3	4	4	3	5	4	3	4	4	4	3	4	2	4	4	3	4	4	66 -283
Toshimitsu Izawa	Round 1	5	3	4	3	5	4	3	5	5	5	6	4	3	4	4	4	4	5	76
Japan	Round 2	4	4	4	3	5	3	3	4	5	4	3	4	3	5	4	3	3	4	68
£32,000	Round 3	5	3	4	3	5	4	3	4	5	4	5	4	4	4	3	3	5	4	72
	Round 4	5	3	3	2	5	4	3	4	4	5	4	5	3	3	4	4	3	4	67 -283
Mark O'Meara	Round 1	4	4	4	3	6	5	3	4	5	4	4	4	2	4	3	3	4	3	69
USA	Round 2	4	4	3	3	6	4	3	4	5	4	4	4	3	4	3	3	5	3	69
£32,000	Round 3	4	4	5	4	6	4	3	4	6	5	4	4	4	4	4	3	5	4	77
	Round 4	3	4	3	2	5	4	3	3	5	4	4	3	3	5	4	3	5	5	68 -283
Corey Pavin	Round 1	4	4	4	3	5	5	3	4	4	4	4	4	3	3	4	3	4	4	69
USA	Round 2	4	4	4	3	4	5	3	3	5	4	4	4	3	4	4	3	4	5	70
£32,000	Round 3	5	4	4	3	5	4	2	5	5	5	4	4	2	5	4	3	7	4	75
	Round 4	3	4	4	3	5	3	3	4	5	4	4	4	3	4	4	3	5	4	69-283
David Duval	Round 1	5	4	4	2	4	5	3	4	4	5	4	4	3	4	4	4	5	4	72
USA	Round 2	5	4	3	2	5	4	3	4	4	4	4	4	2	4	5	3	7	4	71
£32,000	Round 3	5	3	3	3	5	4	3	4	4	4	4	4	3	5	3	3	5	5	70
	Round 4	4	3	4	3	5	5	2	3	7	4	3	4	3	4	5	3	4	4	70-283
Justin Rose	Round 1	4	3	3	3	5	4	3	4	3	5	4	4	3	4	4	3	5	4	68
England	Round 2	5	4	4	5	5	4	3	4	4	5	4	4	3	5	4	3	5	4	75
£32,000	Round 3	4	4	4	3	4	3	3	4	5	5	3	4	3	4	3	3	5	4	68
	Round 4	5	4	4	2	5	6	3	4	4	4	4	4	3	4	4	3	5	4	72 -283
Tiger Woods	Round 1	4	4	4	3	4	5	3	4	4	5	3	4	3	4	4	3	5	4	70
USA	Round 2	4	4	3	3	4	4	3	4	5	4	4	4	3	4	4	3	4	4	68
£24,000	Round 3	5	4	4	4	7	5	3	5	5	5	4	5	5	5	4	3	4	4	81
	Round 4	4	4	5	3	4	3	3	4	3	4	3	4	2	4	3	3	5	4	65 -284
Pierre Fulke	Round 1	4	4	4	3	5	4	3	4	4	5	4	4	4	3	4	4	4	5	72
Sweden	Round 2	4	4	3	3	4	4	3	5	5	4	4	4	3	4	4	3	4	4	69
£24,000	Round 3	4	3	4	4	6	5	3	4	5	4	4	4	4	5	5	3	7	4	78
	Round 4	4	4	4	2	4	4	2	4	5	5	3	3	2	4	5	2	4	4	65 -284
Bradley Dredge	Round 1	4	4	4	3	4	6	3	4	5	5	4	4	3	3	4	2	5	3	70
Wales	Round 2	5	4	5	3	4	4	4	4	4	4	3	4	3	4	5	2	5	5	72
£24,000	Round 3	3	3	4	4	6	5	2	5	5	4	4	4	4	4	5	4	5	3	74
	Round 4	4	4	4	2	4	5	3	4	4	5	3	4	3	3	4	3	6	3	68 -284
Bernhard Langer	Round 1	5	5	4	2	4	4	3	4	6	5	4	3	3	4	4	3	5	4	72
Germany	Round 2	5	4	4	3	5	4	3	4	4	4	4	5	3	4	5	2	5	4	72
£24,000	Round 3	5	4	4	2	4	4	3	3	4	5	4	4	4	5	4	4	4	4	71
	Round 4	5	3	4	3	4	4	3	4	4	4	4	4	3	4	4	3	5	4	69 -284

HOLE		1	2	3	4	5	6	7	8	9	10	11	12	13	14	15	16	17	18	
PAR		4	4	4	3	5	4	3	4	5	4	4	4	3	4	4	3	5	4	TOTAL
Niclas Fasth	Round 1	4	4	4	3	4	4	3	4	5	5	4	4	3	4	4	4	3	4	70
Sweden	Round 2	5	5	3	3	5	6	3	4	5	4	4	3	3	5	3	3	4	5	73
£24,000	Round 3	5	3	4	3	5	4	3	4	5	4	4	4	3	3	4	3	6	4	71
	Round 4	4	3	3	3	5	4	3	5	4	5	5	4	3	4	4	3	4	4	70 -284
Jerry Kelly	Round 1	4	4	5	3	5	4	3	5	4	4	5	4	3	4	4	3	4	5	73
USA	Round 2	5	4	4	3	5	5	3	4	4	4	4	4	3	4	4	3	4	4	71
£24,000	Round 3	3	4	4	3	5	4	3	7	4	4	3	3	3	4	4	3	5	4	70
	Round 4	4	4	4	3	5	5	4	4	4	4	4	4	3	4	3	3	4	4	70 -284
Jesper Parnevik	Round 1	4	3	4	3	7	5	3	4	5	5	4	4	3	4	4	2	5	3	72
Sweden	Round 2	5	5	4	3	4	5	3	4	6	5	4	3	3	4	5	3	3	3	72
£24,000	Round 3	3	3	5	3	4	4	2	4	4	5	4	4	3	5	5	3	5	4	70
	Round 4	5	4	3	3	4	4	3	4	5	4	4	4	3	4	4	2	4	6	70 -284
Loren Roberts	Round 1	5	3	4	3	6	5	3	5	4	5	4	4	4	3	4	3	4	5	74
USA	Round 2	4	4	4	3	4	4	3	4	5	4	3	4	3	5	4	3	4	4	69
£24,000	Round 3	5	4	4	3	5	4	2	4	4	4	4	4	3	4	4	3	4	5	70
	Round 4	4	4	4	3	5	5	3	4	5	4	4	4	3	4	4	3	4	4	71 -284
Des Smyth	Round 1	5	4	4	3	4	3	3	4	5	4	3	4	3	4	4	3	4	4	68
Ireland	Round 2	4	4	4	3	4	4	2	4	4	4	5	4	3	4	4	3	5	4	69
£24,000	Round 3	6	4	4	3	5	4	3	5	4	4	4	3	3	4	3	4	6	5	74
	Round 4	4	4	4	3	5	4	3	4	4	4	4	5	3	4	5	3	5	5	73 -284
Neal Lancaster	Round 1	4	3	5	3	4	4	2	4	4	4	5	4	4	5	4	3	5	4	71
USA	Round 2	3	3	4	3	5	4	3	4	4	5	4	5	2	4	5	4	5	4	71
£16,917	Round 3	5	4	5	3	5	4	3	4	4	5	4	4	4	4	5	3	5	5	76
	Round 4	4	4	4	3	4	4	3	3	4	5	4	3	3	4	4	4	4	3	67 -285
Ian Woosnam	Round 1	4	4	5	3	5	3	3	4	5	4	4	4	3	4	3	4	6	4	72
Wales	Round 2	5	3	3	4	6	4	3	3	5	4	4	4	3	5	4	3	5	4	72
£16,917	Round 3	4	4	3	2	5	5	3	4	5	6	4	4	3	5	4	3	5	4	73
	Round 4	4	4	3	3	5	4	3	4	6	3	4	4	2	4	3	3	5	4	68 -285
Darren Clarke	Round 1	4	4	4	4	5	5	3	4	5	4	4	4	3	4	4	3	4	4	72
N. Ireland	Round 2	3	4	4	2	3	5	3	4	4	3	4	4	3	5	4	3	5	4	67
£16,917	Round 3	3	5	4	4	6	5	5	4	5	4	4	3	4	5	4	4	4	4	77
	Round 4	3	3	4	3	4	4	3	4	5	4	4	5	3	4	4	3	5	4	69 -285
Stephen Leaney	Round 1	4	4	4	4	5	4	2	4	5	4	3	4	2	5	4	3	5	5	71
Australia	Round 2	4	3	4	3	4	3	3	4	4	3	4	5	3	5	5	4	5	4	70
£16,917	Round 3	4	3	3	3	8	4	3	4	4	5	4	4	5	4	4	5	4	4	75
	Round 4	4	4	4	2	4	4	3	4	4	5	4	3	3	4	5	3	5	4	69 -285
Andrew Coltart	Round 1	4	3	4	3	4	5	3	3	4	5	4	5	3	4	4	4	5	4	71
Scotland	Round 2	5	4	4	3	5	4	4	3	4	5	3	3	3	4	3	3	5	4	69
£16,917	Round 3	3	5	4	4	5	4	4	3	5	5	4	4	2	4	4	4	5	5	74
	Round 4	5	4	4	4	5	4	3	4	4	6	4	3	2	4	3	3	4	5	71 -285
Scott Verplank	Round 1	4	4	4	3	5	4	3	5	4	4	4	4	2	5	4	3	6	4	72
USA	Round 2	4	3	3	3	5	5	3	3	4	5	4	4	3	3	4	3	5	4	68
£16,917	Round 3	4	4	4	3	4	4	3	5	5	5	4	4	5	2	4	3	5	6	74
	Round 4	4	4	4	3	4	4	3	4	5	5	4	4	3	4	4	4	4	4	71 -285
Esteban Toledo	Round 1	4	4	4	3	5	6	3	4	5	4	4	4	4	4	3	3	4	5	73
Mexico	Round 2	5	4	4	4	5	3	2	5	5	4	3	4	3	4	3	3	5	4	70
£13,750	Round 3	4	5	4	3	5	4	3	4	5	5	4	4	3	4	4	3	5	6	75
	Round 4	4	3	5	3	5	4	2	3	4	4	4	3	3	4	5	2	4	6	68-286

HOLE		1	2	3	4	5	6	7	8	9	10	11	12	13	14	15	16	17	18	
PAR		4	4	4	3	5	4	3	4	5	4	4	4	3	4	4	3	5	4	TOTAL
Steve Jones	Round 1	4	4	4	4	4	4	3	4	4	4	4	4	3	4	3	3	3	5	68
USA	Round 2	5	5	3	3	5	6	2	4	4	4	3	5	4	5	4	3	5	5	75
£13,750	Round 3	4	4	4	3	5	4	3	5	3	4	4	5	3	4	5	3	6	4	73
	Round 4	4	4	4	3	5	3	4	4	5	4	4	4	2	4	4	3	5	4	70 -286
Trevor Immelman	Round 1	4	4	5	3	5	4	3	5	4	4	4	4	4	4	4	3	4	4	72
South Africa	Round 2	5	5	4	3	4	5	2	4	5	4	4	5	2	4	4	3	5	4	72
£13,750	Round 3	5	4	3	3	4	4	4	3	4	5	4	4	3	4	5	2	5	5	71
	Round 4	4	4	3	2	4	4	5	4	5	5	4	4	3	3	4	3	5	5	71 -286
Carl Pettersson	Round 1	4	4	3	3	4	4	3	4	4	4	3	4	3	5	3	3	4	5	67
Sweden	Round 2	4	3	4	3	4	4	4	4	5	4	4	4	3	4	4	3	5	4	70
£13,750	Round 3	4	5	5	3	4	4	3	5	5	4	4	4	3	4	4	3	6	6	76
	Round 4	4	4	4	3	5	4	5	4	4	4	4	4	3	5	4	3	5	4	73 -286
Paul Eales	Round 1	4	4	5	3	5	4	3	5	4	5	4	4	3	4	4	3	5	4	73
England	Round 2	3	4	4	3	6	4	2	5	4	6	3	4	3	4	4	3	5	4	71
£12,000	Round 3	4	4	4	4	5	5	3	4	5	5	4	3	4	4	5	3	5	5	76
	Round 4	4	4	4	3	4	4	2	4	4	3	3	4	4	3	3	4	5	5	67 -287
Jeff Maggert	Round 1	5	3	4	3	4	3	3	4	4	4	4	5	3	3	5	4	5	5	71
USA	Round 2	4	4	3	3	5	4	4	3	4	4	4	3	3	5	3	3	5	4	68
£12,000	Round 3	4	4	4	2	5	4	3	4	6	6	5	4	3	5	4	4	7	6	80
	Round 4	4	4	3	3	4	4	3	5	4	5	3	4	3	4	4	3	4	4	68 -287
Rocco Mediate	Round 1	5	3	5	3	5	4	3	4	4	4	4	4	4	4	4	3	4	4	71
USA	Round 2	4	4	4	3	4	5	3	4	5	4	4	4	5	4	4	3	4	4	72
£12,000	Round 3	5	5	5	3	4	4	3	3	5	5	4	3	3	4	4	4	5	5	74
	Round 4	4	4	4	3	5	4	3	4	4	4	3	5	2	5	4	3	5	4	70 -287
Warren Bennett	Round 1	5	4	4	4	4	4	3	5	3	4	4	4	3	4	4	3	5	4	71
England	Round 2	4	4	4	3	6	3	3	5	5	3	3	4	3	4	4	2	4	4	68
£10,267	Round 3	5	4	4	4	7	5	3	5	5	5	4	5	4	4	4	3	6	5	82
	Round 4	5	3	3	3	5	4	3	3	5	4	4	4	2	5	3	2	5	4	67 -288
Mikko Ilonen	Round 1	5	3	4	2	5	5	3	4	5	4	4	4	2	5	4	4	4	4	71
Finland	Round 2	4	3	4	4	3	5	3	3	5	5	5	4	2	4	4	3	5	4	70
£10,267	Round 3	3	4	4	3	5	8	3	5	5	5	6	5	3	3	4	2	5	4	77
	Round 4	5	4	4	3	5	4	4	4	5	4	4	4	2	4	4	2	4	4	70 -288
Fredrik Andersson	Round 1	6	3	4	3	5	5	3	5	4	4	4	4	4	3	4	4	5	4	74
Sweden	Round 2	5	3	4	3	4	4	2	3	4	4	5	4	3	5	3	4	5	5	70
£10,267	Round 3	5	4	4	4	5	4	3	5	4	4	4	4	3	4	4	3	6	4	74
	Round 4	4	3	4	3	6	4	2	4	4	4	4	4	4	5	3	3	5	4	70 -288
Ian Poulter	Round 1	5	4	4	3	5	5	2	4	5	4	4	4	2	4	4	2	4	4	69
England	Round 2	5	3	4	3	5	4	2	4	4	4	4	4	3	4	4	3	5	4	69
£10,267	Round 3	5	4	5	3	6	6	3	4	4	5	5	4	4	5	4	2	4	5	78
	Round 4	6	4	3	4	5	4	3	3	4	4	4	4	3	5	5	2	4	5	72 -288
Bob Tway	Round 1	4	4	4	3	5	4	3	4	4	4	4	4	3	4	4	4	4	4	70
USA	Round 2	4	4	3	2	4	5	3	4	4	4	3	4	3	4	4	3	4	4	66
£10,267	Round 3	6	5	4	4	4	5	3	5	4	4	4	4	5	4	5	3	5	4	78
	Round 4	5	3	4	4	5	4	3	4	5	4	4	4	3	4	4	4	5	5	74 -288
Shingo Katayama	Round 1	4	4	4	3	5	3	3	4	5	5	4	4	3	4	4	4	5	4	72
Japan	Round 2	4	4	3	3	4	5	4	3	4	4	4	4	2	4	4	4	4	4	68
£10,267	Round 3	4	4	3	4	5	5	3	4	4	6	5	3	3	4	5	3	5	4	74
	Round 4	7	4	4	3	4	5	4	3	5	5	4	3	4	5	3	3	4	4	74 -288

HOLE		1	2	3	4	5	6	7	8	9	10	11	12	13	14	15	16	17	18	
PAR		4	4	4	3	5	4	3	4	5	4	4	4	3	4	4	3	5	4	TOTAL
Barry Lane	Round 1	4	4	4	3	4	5	4	4	4	5	4	4	3	4	4	3	5	6	74
England	Round 2	4	4	4	2	5	4	3	3	6	4	3	4	2	6	4	2	4	4	68
£10,267	Round 3	6	3	4	3	5	4	3	5	4	4	4	4	3	4	4	4	4	4	72
	Round 4	5	4	4	4	5	3	3	4	5	5	4	4	3	5	4	4	4	4	74-288
Ian Garbutt	Round 1	3	4	4	3	5	4	3	4	5	4	4	3	3	4	5	3	4	4	69
England	Round 2	4	4	4	2	5	5	3	4	4	5	3	5	3	3	4	3	5	4	70
£10,267	Round 3	5	4	3	4	5	5	3	4	5	5	5	4	2	3	4	3	5	5	74
	Round 4	5	4	4	2	4	4	3	4	5	4	4	4	5	6	5	2	5	5	75-288
Craig Perks	Round 1	5	4	4	3	4	4	3	5	4	5	4	4	3	5	4	3	4	4	72
New Zealand	Round 2	4	4	4	3	5	4	3	4	5	4	4	4	2	4	4	4	4	4	70
£10,267	Round 3	4	3	4	4	4	4	3	3	4	5	3	4	3	4	4	4	6	5	71
	Round 4	4	4	4	4	5	4	3	5	4	6	4	3	4	5	4	3	4	5	75-288
Steve Stricker	Round 1	4	4	3	2	5	5	3	4	5	4	4	5	2	5	3	4	4	3	69
USA	Round 2	4	3	5	4	3	4	2	4	5	4	4	4	3	5	3	3	6	4	70
£9,300	Round 3	4	5	4	3	8	5	5	4	4	5	5	4	3	4	5	3	5	5	81
	Round 4	4	4	4	4	4	5	3	3	4	4	4	4	2	4	4	3	4	5	69-289
Stewart Cink	Round 1	3	3	4	3	4	5	3	4	6	4	4	4	4	4	5	2	5	4	71
USA	Round 2	4	4	4	3	3	4	3	4	5	4	4	4	3	4	4	3	4	5	69
£9,300	Round 3	4	4	6	3	6	7	3	5	4	4	5	3	4	4	4	4	5	5	80
	Round 4	5	4	4	4	4	3	3	4	4	3	4	3	3	5	4	4	4	4	69-289
Richard Green	Round 1	4	4	4	3	7	5	3	4	4	4	4	3	3	4	3	4	5	4	72
Australia	Round 2	4	4	3	3	7	3	4	5	5	3	5	4	3	4	3	3	5	4	72
£9,300	Round 3	4	5	4	4	6	4	3	4	4	5	4	5	3	4	5	3	4	4	75
	Round 4	4	4	4	3	5	6	3	4	4	5	3	4	2	4	4	3	4	4	70-289
Paul Lawrie	Round 1	4	4	3	3	5	4	3	4	4	5	4	4	3	3	4	4	5	4	70
Scotland	Round 2	5	4	3	5	5	4	3	3	4	4	3	4	3	4	5	3	4	4	70
£9,300	Round 3	4	6	4	3	6	4	3	3	6	5	5	4	4	4	5	3	5	4	78
	Round 4	4	4	4	4	5	3	4	4	3	5	4	4	3	4	4	3	5	4	71-289
Nick Faldo	Round 1	4	4	4	3	5	5	4	4	5	5	3	4	3	4	3	3	5	5	73
England	Round 2	4	4	4	3	3	3	3	5	4	4	4	4	3	5	4	3	5	4	69
£9,300	Round 3	5	4	3	3	5	6	4	4	5	4	4	4	4	4	4	4	5	4	76
	Round 4	4	4	4	3	6	4	3	3	4	4	4	4	3	5	4	3	4	5	71-289
Kenichi Kuboya	Round 1	4	4	4	3	5	5	3	4	4	4	4	4	3	4	4	3	4	4	70
Japan	Round 2	6	4	4	4	3	4	3	4	5	4	4	4	3	3	5	4	4	5	73
£9,300	Round 3	5	3	4	3	5	3	3	4	5	5	5	4	3	4	4	3	5	6	73
	Round 4	4	4	4	4	5	7	2	3	4	4	4	4	3	4	5	3	5	4	73-289
Joe Durant	Round 1	4	4	4	3	4	5	4	5	4	4	4	4	3	4	4	3	5	4	72
USA	Round 2	3	5	4	3	5	4	4	4	5	5	4	4	3	3	4	3	4	4	71
£9,300	Round 3	4	4	4	2	4	4	3	4	4	5	4	4	3	5	4	4	6	5	73
	Round 4	4	4	4	3	4	4	4	5	5	5	4	4	3	4	3	3	5	5	73-289
Phil Mickelson	Round 1	4	4	5	3	5	4	2	4	5	4	4	4	2	4	4	3	4	3	68
USA	Round 2	6	3	4	4	5	5	3	4	5	4	4	4	3	6	5	3	4	4	76
£8,800	Round 3	5	4	4	3	6	5	3	5	6	4	4	5	4	3	4	3	4	4	76
	Round 4	4	3	4	3	5	4	3	4	5	4	4	3	3	4	4	3	5	5	70-290
Jarrod Moseley	Round 1	5	4	4	3	5	4	3	4	4	4	4	4	3	4	4	3	4	4	70
Australia	Round 2	4	4	4	3	4	5	3	4	5	5	4	4	3	4	5	3	5	4	73
£8,800	Round 3	6	3	5	3	5	4	3	4	5	4	4	4	5	5	4	3	4	4	75
	Round 4	5	4	4	3	4	4	3	4	5	4	4	4	3	5	4	3	4	5	72-290

HOLE		1	2	3	4	5	6	7	8	9	10	11	12	13	14	15	16	17	18	
PAR		4	4	4	3	5	4	3	4	5	4	4	4	3	4	4	3	5	4	TOTAL
Chris DiMarco	Round 1	5	4	4	3	5	4	3	3	4	4	5	4	3	4	4	3	5	5	72
USA	Round 2	4	3	3	3	4	3	4	4	4	4	4	4	6	4	4	3	4	4	69
£8,800	Round 3	4	4	3	3	5	5	3	4	5	5	5	3	4	4	4	3	6	5	75
	Round 4	4	4	4	3	5	4	3	4	5	4	4	5	3	4	5	4	5	4	74 -290
Matthew Cort	Round 1	5	4	4	4	5	4	3	4	5	3	3	4	3	5	5	3	5	4	73
England	Round 2	4	4	4	3	5	6	3	4	5	4	3	4	3	5	3	2	5	4	71
£8,517	Round 3	5	3	4	3	5	5	3	4	5	5	4	5	3	6	5	3	5	5	78
	Round 4	4	3	4	3	5	4	2	4	5	5	4	4	2	6	4	2	4	4	69 -291
Toru Taniguchi	Round 1	5	4	3	3	4	3	3	5	4	5	4	4	4	4	4	3	5	4	71
Japan	Round 2	5	5	4	4	5	4	4	4	4	5	4	3	3	4	3	4	4	5	73
£8,517	Round 3	5	4	4	3	5	4	3	4	4	4	4	4	3	5	5	3	6	6	76
	Round 4	4	4	4	3	4	5	3	4	4	6	4	4	3	4	4	3	5	3	71 -291
Stephen Ames	Round 1	5	3	5	3	5	4	3	5	4	4	3	4	2	5	4	2	4	3	68
Trinidad & Tobago	Round 2	4	4	4	3	3	4	2	5	5	5	3	4	3	5	4	3	5	4	70
£8,517	Round 3	5	4	5	7	5	5	4	4	5	5	5	4	4	4	4	2	5	4	81
	Round 4	4	4	4	3	4	5	4	4	4	5	4	3	3	4	4	3	6	4	72 -291
Len Mattiace	Round 1	3	4	4	3	5	5	3	4	4	3	4	4	3	5	3	3	4	4	68
USA	Round 2	5	3	4	3	5	5	2	3	6	5	4	4	3	4	4	3	5	5	73
£8,517	Round 3	4	4	3	3	6	4	3	4	4	6	5	4	4	4	4	4	6	5	77
	Round 4	4	4	4	3	5	5	3	5	4	4	4	4	2	4	5	3	6	4	73 -291
Jim Carter	Round 1	5	4	4	4	6	4	2	4	4	4	5	4	3	4	5	4	4	4	74
USA	Round 2	4	4	4	3	5	4	3	4	4	4	3	5	4	4	3	3	4	5	70
£8,517	Round 3	5	5	4	3	5	5	3	4	4	5	4	4	3	4	3	4	4	4	73
	Round 4	6	4	4	4	4	4	3	4	5	5	4	4	3	5	4	2	5	4	74 -291
Mike Weir	Round 1	5	4	3	4	5	4	3	5	4	4	5	3	4	4	4	3	5	4	73
Canada	Round 2	4	4	4	3	5	4	3	4	3	5	3	4	4	4	4	3	4	4	69
£8,517	Round 3	5	3	3	3	5	4	3	4	4	4	4	4	3	5	4	4	8	4	74
	Round 4	4	4	3	3	6	4	3	4	4	4	4	4	5	5	4	3	6	4	75 -291
Sandy Lyle	Round 1	4	3	3	4	5	4	4	4	5	4	3	4	4	4	4	2	4	3	68
Scotland	Round 2	5	4	5	4	6	4	2	4	6	4	3	3	4	5	4	4	5	4	76
£8,500	Round 3	6	4	5	3	5	4	3	3	5	4	4	4	3	4	4	3	5	4	73
	Round 4	5	4	4	3	5	4	3	4	5	4	4	4	3	5	4	4	4	6	75 -292
Chris Smith	Round 1	4	5	3	3	6	4	3	4	4	5	4	4	2	4	4	3	8	4	74
USA	Round 2	4	4	3	3	5	5	3	4	4	4	4	4	3	3	4	4	4	4	69
£8,500	Round 3	4	4	3	3	5	5	2	4	5	5	3	4	3	4	4	4	5	4	71
	Round 4	5	4	5	3	5	4	4	4	5	4	4	4	3	5	4	4	6	5	78 -292
Anders Hansen	Round 1	6	4	4	4	5	3	3	4	3	5	4	4	3	4	4	3	4	4	71
Denmark	Round 2	5	4	4	3	5	6	3	4	4	4	3	4	3	4	4	4	4	4	72
£8,500	Round 3	5	4	4	3	5	3	3	6	5	5	4	4	4	4	5	4	7	4	79
	Round 4	5	4	3	4	5	4	3	4	5	4	3	3	3	5	4	3	5	4	71 -293
Roger Wessels	Round 1	5	4	4	2	6	4	3	4	4	4	4	4	3	4	4	4	4	5	72
South Africa	Round 2	4	3	4	3	5	5	2	4	5	4	4	4	3	4	5	3	4	5	71
£8,500	Round 3	4	4	5	4	4	3	3	4	6	4	4	4	4	4	4	3	5	4	73
	Round 4	5	4	4	4	6	4	4	4	4	5	5	3	4	4	6	3	4	4	77 -293
David Park	Round 1	3	4	5	3	6	4	4	4	4	4	6	3	2	4	4	4	4	5	73
Wales	Round 2	4	4	4	3	4	4	3	4	5	5	3	4	2	4	4	3	4	3	67
£8,500	Round 3	4	4	4	3	6	4	3	4	4	4	3	4	4	4	5	4	6	4	74
	Round 4	5	4	4	3	4	5	3	4	5	4	4	4	11	4	4	4	4	4	80 -294

HOLE		1	2	3	4	5	6	7	8	9	10	11	12	13	14	15	16	17	18	
PAR		4	4	4	3	5	4	3	4	5	4	4	4	3	4	4	3	5	4	TOTAL
Lee Janzen	Round 1	4	5	4	3	4	4	3	5	4	4	3	4	3	4	4	3	5	4	70
USA	Round 2	5	4	3	3	4	4	2	4	5	4	4	5	3	4	4	3	4	4	69
£8,500	Round 3	5	4	6	4	7	5	3	5	4	5	4	4	5	4	4	4	6	5	84
	Round 4	5	3	4	4	5	3	3	4	4	5	4	3	3	4	5	3	4	6	72 -295
Mark Calcavecchia	Round 1	4	3	3	4	6	4	3	4	5	4	3	4	4	6	4	4	4	5	74
USA	Round 2	3	4	3	4	4	3	3	4	4	5	3	3	4	4	4	3	4	4	66
£8,500	Round 3	3	4	5	3	5	4	3	4	5	5	4	4	4	7	6	5	6	4	81
	Round 4	4	4	4	3	6	4	3	4	5	5	4	3	4	4	4	3	5	5	74 -295
Colin Montgomerie	Round 1	4	3	3	3	6	4	3	6	4	4	4	4	3	6	4	3	5	5	74
Scotland	Round 2	3	4	4	3	3	3	3	4	4	4	4	4	3	4	3	3	5	3	64
£8,500	Round 3	4	4	4	4	6	5	3	6	5	6	5	5	4	4	4	4	6	5	84
	Round 4	4	4	4	3	5	4	4	4	5	5	3	4	4	5	5	3	5	4	75 -297
David Toms	Round 1	4	4	3	2	5	4	3	4	5	4	4	3	2	5	4	3	4	4	67
USA	Round 2	6	4	4	3	5	5	4	4	4	4	5	4	3	5	3	3	5	4	75
£8,500	Round 3	4	4	4	3	4	6	3	8	4	5	4	4	4	5	4	4	6	5	81
	Round 4	4	4	5	4	5	4	3	3	5	5	3	4	3	5	5	4	5	4	75 -298

NON QUALIFIERS AFTER 36 HOLES

(Leading 10 professionals and ties receive £3,000 each, next 20 professionals and ties receive £2,500 each, next 20 professionals and ties receive £2,250 each, remainder of professionals receive £2,000 each.)

HOLE		1	2	3	4	5	6	7	8	9	10	11	12	13	14	15	16	17	18	
PAR		4	4	4	3	5	4	3	4	5	4	4	4	3	4	4	3	5	4	TOTAL
Michael Campbell	Round 1	5	4	4	2	4	5	4	4	4	3	4	6	3	5	4	4	5	4	74
New Zealand	Round 2	5	3	4	4	5	4	3	4	5	4	4	4	3	4	4	3	4	4	71 -145
Matt Kuchar	Round 1	4	4	4	4	5	5	3	5	5	4	4	4	3	4	4	3	5	5	75
USA	Round 2	4	4	3	3	6	4	3	5	4	4	3	4	3	4	4	3	5	4	70 -145
Jose Maria Olazabal	Round 1	4	4	4	4	5	4	3	4	5	4	4	3	3	5	4	3	5	5	73
Spain	Round 2	5	3	4	3	4	4	4	5	5	4	4	3	3	4	4	4	5	4	72 -145
John Bickerton	Round 1	5	4	3	3	5	5	3	5	4	5	4	4	3	4	3	4	5	4	73
England	Round 2	4	4	3	3	5	6	2	4	6	4	5	4	3	4	4	3	4	4	72 -145
Marc Farry	Round 1	4	5	4	3	4	4	3	4	4	4	4	4	3	5	4	2	5	4	70
France	Round 2	4	4	4	3	5	5	3	4	5	4	4	6	3	5	4	3	4	5	75 -145
Magnus Persson	Round 1	6	3	3	3	6	4	3	5	4	4	3	4	3	4	4	3	6	4	72
Sweden	Round 2	3	4	4	4	6	5	3	4	4	4	4	4	3	4	4	4	5	4	73 -145
Lee Westwood	Round 1	5	3	4	3	5	5	3	4	5	4	4	5	3	4	4	3	4	4	72
England	Round 2	4	5	4	2	5	4	3	4	4	4	4	4	3	5	4	3	6	5	73 -145
Brad Faxon	Round 1	4	3	4	3	4	4	3	4	4	4	5	4	3	5	4	4	5	3	70
USA	Round 2	5	4	5	3	5	4	3	3	4	5	4	4	4	4	5	3	5	5	75 -145
Eduardo Romero	Round 1	4	4	4	2	5	5	2	5	4	4	4	4	4	4	4	4	5	4	72
Argentina	Round 2	5	4	4	4	4	3	4	4	4	4	3	4	3	4	5	3	5	6	73 -145

HOLE		1	2	3	4	5	6	7	8	9	10	11	12	13	14	15	16	17	18	
PAR		4	4	4	3	5	4	3	4	5	4	4	4	3	4	4	3	5	4	TOTAL
Adam Scott	Round 1	5	4	5	3	5	6	3	5	4	5	4	4	4	4	4	3	5	4	77
Australia	Round 2	4	4	4	3	5	4	3	4	5	4	3	4	3	4	3	3	4	4	68 -145
Jean-Francois Remesy	Round 1	5	3	4	2	5	5	3	4	4	4	4	3	2	5	3	3	4	5	68
France	Round 2	4	4	4	4	5	4	3	4	5	4	5	5	5	4	4	3	5	5	77 -145
Alex Cejka	Round 1	4	4	4	4	6	5	3	5	3	4	4	4	3	4	4	3	5	4	73
Germany	Round 2	5	4	3	4	4	4	3	4	6	5	3	4	3	4	4	3	5	5	73 -146
Taichi Teshima	Round 1	4	4	4	4	5	4	3	4	4	4	3	3	3	4	5	2	5	4	69
Japan	Round 2	4	5	4	4	4	4	3	4	4	6	6	5	3	4	4	3	4	6	77-146
Tim Clark	Round 1	5	3	4	3	4	5	3	5	4	4	4	4	2	5	3	3	5	4	70
South Africa	Round 2	6	5	4	3	5	6	4	4	4	4	4	5	3	4	3	3	5	4	76 -146
Tom Lehman	Round 1	4	4	4	3	4	5	3	3	4	6	4	4	3	4	4	3	5	3	70
USA	Round 2	5	4	4	3	4	5	3	4	6	4	4	4	4	4	4	3	5	4	76 -146
K.J. Choi	Round 1	4	3	4	3	6	4	3	5	5	3	4	5	3	5	5	4	4	3	73
Korea	Round 2	4	4	3	3	5	4	3	4	5	4	4	5	4	5	4	3	5	4	73 -146
Tom Whitehouse	Round 1	5	3	5	3	5	5	3	5	5	4	3	4	4	5	4	4	4	4	75
England	Round 2	4	3	5	3	5	5	4	4	5	3	4	3	3	4	4	3	5	4	71 -146
Billy Mayfair	Round 1	4	3	5	4	4	4	3	4	4	4	4	4	3	5	4	3	4	5	71
USA	Round 2	4	4	4	3	5	5	3	5	5	4	4	5	4	4	4	3	4	5	75 -146
Tim Petrovic	Round 1	5	4	4	3	5	4	4	4	4	4	5	4	3	3	5	3	5	4	73
USA	Round 2	4	3	4	3	4	4	3	4	6	5	4	4	3	5	4	3	5	5	73 -146
John Senden	Round 1	4	3	4	3	7	4	4	4	4	6	3	4	3	4	3	5	6	5	76
Australia	Round 2	3	4	5	3	6	5	5	3	4	3	4	4	3	4	4	3	3	4	70 -146
Paul McGinley	Round 1	5	4	4	3	6	4	3	5	4	4	3	4	4	3	4	3	5	4	72
Ireland	Round 2	6	3	4	3	4	4	3	5	5	4	4	4	4	4	5	3	5	4	74 -146
Craig Parry	Round 1	4	4	4	3	5	4	3	4	5	4	3	4	3	5	5	3	5	4	72
Australia	Round 2	5	4	3	4	4	5	3	4	5	4	5	4	4	4	4	3	4	4	74 -146
Robert Karlsson	Round 1	4	4	4	3	5	4	3	4	5	4	3	4	4	4	5	4	4	4	72
Sweden	Round 2	5	3	4	3	5	5	3	5	5	4	4	3	3	3	4	4	5	6	74 -146
Scott Henderson	Round 1	5	3	4	5	7	4	3	4	6	4	3	4	3	4	5	5	5	4	78
Scotland	Round 2	4	3	4	3	3	4	3	4	4	4	4	4	3	5	4	4	5	3	68 -146
Luke Donald	Round 1	5	4	4	3	7	4	3	4	4	4	3	4	3	4	3	3	6	5	73
England	Round 2	5	4	4	3	5	6	3	4	5	3	5	4	4	4	5	3	4	3	74 -147
Mathias Gronberg	Round 1	4	4	5	3	4	4	2	4	5	4	4	4	3	4	5	3	6	7	75
Sweden	Round 2	4	4	5	3	4	4	3	4	5	4	4	4	2	5	4	3	5	4	72-147
Robert Allenby	Round 1	5	4	4	4	7	4	3	4	4	4	4	4	3	4	4	3	4	4	73
Australia	Round 2	6	5	4	3	5	4	3	3	4	4	4	4	3	4	4	4	6	4	74 -147
Tsuneyuki Nakajima	Round 1	5	3	4	3	5	4	3	4	4	5	4	4	4	4	5	4	5	5	75
Japan	Round 2	4	4	4	3	5	4	3	4	4	4	4	4	3	4	4	3	7	4	72 -147
Vijay Singh	Round 1	4	4	4	3	5	4	3	4	4	4	5	4	3	4	4	3	5	5	72
Fiji	Round 2	5	4	4	4	5	5	3	4	5	5	4	4	3	5	4	4	4	3	75 -147
Jim Furyk	Round 1	4	4	5	3	5	4	3	4	5	4	4	4	3	4	4	3	4	4	71
USA	Round 2	4	4	4	3	4	5	3	4	7	4	4	5	3	5	5	3	4	5	76 -147
David Howell	Round 1	5	4	4	3	5	4	4	4	4	4	6	4	3	4	3	3	5	4	73
England	Round 2	4	5	4	3	5	5	4	4	3	4	4	5	3	4	4	3	5	5	74 -147
Raphael Jacquelin	Round 1	4	3	4	3	6	4	3	5	4	4	5	4	4	4	4	3	6	4	74
France	Round 2	4	5	4	3	4	3	3	4	4	5	4	5	4	4	6	2	5	4	73 -147
Scott Laycock	Round 1	4	4	3	4	5	4	3	5	4	3	5	4	3	4	4	4	6	4	73
Australia	Round 2	5	4	4	4	4	4	3	4	4	4	4	4	4	5	4	4	5	4	74 -147

HOLE		1	2	3	4	5	6	7	8	9	10	11	12	13	14	15	16	17	18	
PAR		4	4	4	3	5	4	3	4	5	4	4	4	3	4	4	3	5	4	TOTAL
*Simon Young	Round 1	4	4	5	4	5	3	3	5	4	5	5	5	3	4	6	3	4	4	76
England	Round 2	4	5	4	3	4	3	3	5	6	4	3	4	3	3	5	3	5	4	71 -147
Jose Coceres	Round 1	4	4	4	4	4	4	2	5	4	4	4	4	3	4	4	3	4	5	70
Argentina	Round 2	5	5	4	4	5	4	3	3	5	4	4	5	3	5	4	3	6	6	78 -148
Greg Owen	Round 1	4	4	5	4	6	4	3	4	7	4	4	4	3	4	5	2	6	3	76
England	Round 2	4	4	3	3	4	3	3	5	5	4	5	4	3	6	6	2	5	3	72 -148
Andrew Oldcorn	Round 1	4	4	4	3	4	5	5	5	5	4	4	4	3	5	4	4	8	4	79
Scotland	Round 2	4	4	4	2	5	6	3	4	4	4	4	4	3	4	3	3	5	3	69 -148
*John Kemp	Round 1	4	4	4	3	6	4	3	4	5	4	5	4	3	5	5	3	4	4	74
England	Round 2	4	5	4	4	5	4	3	5	4	4	5	3	4	4	5	3	4	4	74 -148
Ian Stanley	Round 1	5	5	4	3	5	4	3	6	5	5	3	4	4	4	4	3	5	4	76
Australia	Round 2	5	4	3	3	5	5	3	4	5	4	4	4	4	4	4	3	4	4	72 -148
Ricardo Gonzalez	Round 1	5	4	4	3	5	5	3	4	6	4	4	4	4	4	4	3	5	5	76
Argentina	Round 2	5	3	4	4	4	5	3	4	4	4	4	4	3	5	4	3	4	5	72 -148
Miguel Angel Jimenez	Round 1	4	4	4	3	6	5	2	4	5	4	4	4	3	4	5	3	5	4	73
Spain	Round 2	5	5	5	3	5	5	3	4	4	4	4	4	3	5	4	3	5	4	75 -148
Phillip Price	Round 1	6	3	4	3	4	6	3	4	4	5	5	4	3	5	5	3	4	4	75
Wales	Round 2	5	4	4	3	4	5	3	4	7	4	4	4	3	5	4	4	4	3	74 -149
Hal Sutton	Round 1	6	4	3	3	5	5	3	4	4	4	4	4	3	4	4	3	6	5	74
USA	Round 2	5	3	4	3	4	4	4	4	5	3	5	4	3	4	6	3	6	5	75 -149
Adam Mednick	Round 1	4	5	4	5	5	3	3	4	4	4	5	4	3	5	5	3	5	4	75
Sweden	Round 2	5	4	4	4	5	5	3	4	5	4	3	4	3	4	4	4	5	4	74 -149
Benn Barham	Round 1	5	3	4	3	5	5	3	5	6	4	5	3	4	5	4	3	5	4	76
England	Round 2	4	4	4	3	4	5	3	4	4	4	4	5	4	3	5	3	6	4	73 -149
Raymond Russell	Round 1	4	4	3	4	4	5	4	5	4	4	4	3	3	4	4	3	4	5	71
Scotland	Round 2	5	4	4	3	4	5	7	4	5	4	4	5	5	4	4	3	5	4	79 -150
Frank Lickliter II	Round 1	5	4	4	4	5	4	3	4	5	5	4	3	4	5	4	3	4	4	74
USA	Round 2	3	4	4	3	5	4	3	3	8	4	4	5	4	4	5	3	5	5	76 -150
John Cook	Round 1	3	3	5	4	4	5	4	4	4	5	4	4	4	4	4	3	6	4	74
USA	Round 2	4	4	4	3	5	3	3	5	4	7	4	4	3	6	4	3	6	4	76 -150
Dean Wilson	Round 1	4	3	4	4	4	4	3	4	5	5	3	4	4	4	4	3	5	4	71
USA	Round 2	4	3	3	3	7	8	3	4	5	6	4	4	3	5	5	3	5	4	79 -150
Paul Casey	Round 1	4	3	3	4	6	4	3	4	4	5	4	4	3	4	4	3	5	5	72
England	Round 2	6	5	4	3	6	6	4	4	5	4	4	3	4	4	4	3	5	5	78 -150
Darren Fichardt	Round 1	5	3	4	3	6	4	3	4	6	5	4	4	4	5	5	5	5	5	80
South Africa	Round 2	4	4	3	3	4	5	4	4	5	3	4	4	3	4	4	4	4	4	70 -150
Mattias Eliasson	Round 1	5	4	4	3	5	5	3	5	5	5	4	4	3	4	4	5	6	4	78
Sweden	Round 2	5	4	4	4	4	4	3	5	5	4	3	4	3	4	4	3	5	4	72 -150
Kevin Sutherland	Round 1	5	4	4	4	5	3	4	5	4	4	4	4	3	4	4	3	5	4	73
USA	Round 2	5	5	4	3	4	5	3	4	4	6	4	5	3	5	7	3	4	4	78 -151
Toru Suzuki	Round 1	4	4	4	3	5	4	3	5	6	5	5	4	3	5	5	4	5	5	79
Japan	Round 2	4	4	4	3	6	5	3	4	5	4	4	5	2	5	4	3	4	3	72 -151
Gary Emerson	Round 1	5	4	4	5	5	5	2	5	4	4	4	4	3	5	4	3	5	4	75
England	Round 2	4	5	4	3	5	4	4	3	6	5	4	6	3	4	4	4	4	4	76 -151
Peter Baker	Round 1	5	4	4	3	5	4	3	4	5	5	4	5	3	5	5	3	4	4	75
England	Round 2	5	3	4	3	5	4	3	6	4	5	4	5	3	4	5	4	5	4	76 -151
Patrik Sjoland	Round 1	4	3	4	4	5	3	2	5	6	5	4	4	3	4	3	3	7	6	75
Sweden	Round 2	4	3	3	3	5	4	3	5	5	4	3	4	5	7	5	3	6	4	76 -151

HOLE		1	2	3	4	5	6	7	8	9	10	11	12	13	14	15	16	17	18	
PAR		4	4	4	3	5	4	3	4	5	4	4	4	3	4	4	3	5	4	TOTAL
Dudley Hart	Round 1	4	4	4	3	4	4	5	5	4	6	5	4	3	3	4	4	5	3	74
USA	Round 2	5	4	3	6	5	5	3	4	5	6	4	4	3	4	4	4	4	4	77 -151
Fredrik Jacobson	Round 1	5	4	4	4	5	5	4	6	5	4	4	3	3	6	4	3	4	5	78
Sweden	Round 2	4	4	4	5	5	4	3	3	5	5	4	5	3	4	4	4	4	3	73 -151
John Daly	Round 1	5	4	4	3	5	4	3	4	5	4	3	4	4	5	4	4	4	5	74
USA	Round 2	5	4	3	3	5	5	5	5	5	4	4	4	3	5	5	2	5	5	77 -151
Malcolm Mackenzie	Round 1	5	4	4	4	4	4	4	4	4	5	3	4	3	5	4	3	8	4	76
England	Round 2	4	6	4	2	6	4	3	4	6	5	4	4	3	5	4	3	5	4	76-152
Billy Andrade	Round 1	5	3	4	4	5	4	3	4	4	6	5	5	4	4	5	4	4	4	77
USA	Round 2	5	4	5	4	5	3	2	5	5	4	4	5	3	5	3	4	5	4	75 -152
*Alejandro Larrazabal	Round 1	4	4	3	4	5	5	3	4	6	5	5	5	2	4	4	4	5	5	77
Spain	Round 2	4	3	4	2	6	4	3	4	5	5	4	5	4	5	5	3	5	4	75 -152
Angel Cabrera	Round 1	4	4	3	3	5	4	3	6	4	4	4	5	2	5	5	3	5	4	73
Argentina	Round 2	5	4	3	5	6	4	3	4	6	5	4	4	3	4	4	3	6	6	79 -152
John Riegger	Round 1	4	4	5	3	5	4	3	4	4	5	6	4	3	6	4	3	5	6	78
USA	Round 2	4	4	3	3	4	5	4	4	5	5	3	3	3	4	7	3	6	4	74 -152
Jamie Spence	Round 1	4	4	4	4	5	6	3	5	4	5	4	4	4	5	5	3	5	3	77
England	Round 2	5	4	3	3	6	4	3	5	5	4	3	5	3	5	6	3	5	6	78 -155
Tom Watson	Round 1	6	3	4	5	5	5	3	4	4	7	3	4	4	4	4	3	5	4	77
USA	Round 2	5	4	4	3	6	6	2	5	5	4	3	4	3	4	5	4	5	6	78-155
Paul Mayoh	Round 1	6	4	4	4	6	5	4	5	5	5	4	6	5	5	4	3	4	5	84
Wales	Round 2	4	4	4	4	5	4	3	5	5	4	4	4	2	4	4	4	5	4	73 -157
James Kingston	Round 1	4	3	5	3	5	4	4	5	5	3	4	4	5	4	4	3	5	6	76
South Africa	Round 2	4	6	4	3	9	4	3	4	5	4	3	5	3	5	5	3	6	5	81 -157
Kiyoshi Miyazato	Round 1	6	4	4	3	5	5	4	5	5	5	4	4	3	4	4	3	5	4	77
Japan	Round 2	6	4	4	3	4	5	2	5	5	6	5	6	3	5	4	5	6	4	82 -159
Roger Chapman	Round 1	4	4	4	4	6	4	3	5	4	5	4	4	2	4	4	3	6	4	74-DQ
England																				
Jonathan Kaye	Round 1	4	4	4	3	5	4	3	4	5	5	3	5	3	5	4	3	6	4	74-DQ
USA																				
Thongchai Jaidee	Round 1	4	4	4	4	5	6	3	5	6	5	5	4	4	5	3	3	5	5	80-WD
Thailand																				

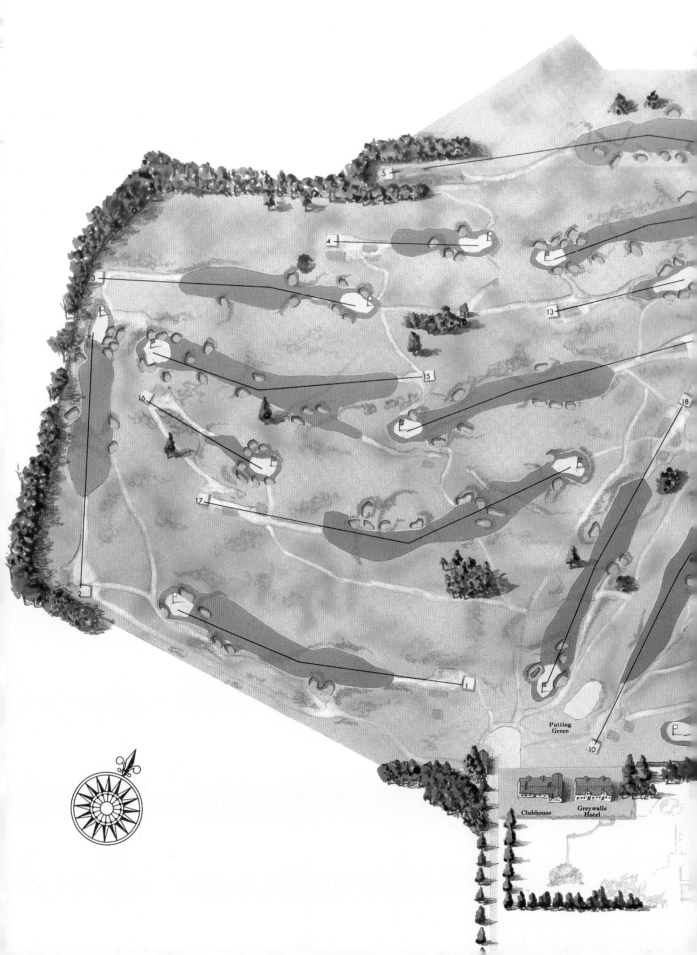

5

4

3

13

15

16

18

17

2

1

10

Putting
Green

Clubhouse   Greywalls
Hotel